QUINE ON ONTOLOGY, NECESSITY, AND EXPERIENCE

The book is a critique of Quine and discusses three interrelated topics which figure prominently in his work. Quine has developed very distinctive views on these topics which are indicated in the title of the book. It criticises these views in some detail and contrasts them with the kind of view which Wittgenstein developed on these topics.

Quine's thought is a well defended fortress in which the different views for which he argues give each other mutual support. Nevertheless it is not impossible to treat a cluster of these in relative isolation from the rest. The present book is an attempt to do just this in the case of the three topics mentioned. It questions some pretty basic assumptions on which the Quinean edifice rests and some of the arguments with which Quine supports these.

The book argues, first, that Quine's whole notion of ontology is riddled with confusion and tries to single out for discussion some of these confusions. It argues, secondly, that Quine's rejection of the distinction between necessary and contingent truths is unwarranted, and that the notion of analyticity in terms of which he conducts this discussion is a red herring. It argues, thirdly, that the notion of experience and the subordinate notion of the senses in terms of which Quine discusses the confirmation of propositions and expounds his brand of empiricism are crude.

Dr İlham Dilman is Reader in Philosophy at the University College of Swansea. He has also taught at the University of California at Los Angeles and Santa Barbara, the University of Oregon at Eugene and the University of Hull.

His books are listed on the next page and he has contributed papers and articles to various philosophical journals and books.

QUINE ON ONTOLOGY, NECESSITY, AND EXPERIENCE

A Philosophical Critique

İlham Dilman

State University of New York Press
Albany

First published in U.S.A. by
State University of New York Press, Albany

Printed in Hong Kong

For information, address State University of New York
Press, State University Plaza, Albany, N.Y., 12246

Library of Congress Cataloging in Publication Data
Dilman, İlham.
Quine on ontology, necessity, and experience.
Bibliography: p.
Includes index.
1. Quine, W. V. (Willard Van Orman) I. Title.
B945.Q54D54   1984   111   83-4815
ISBN 0-87395-761-X
ISBN 0-8739-960-1 (PBK)

Contents

Preface   vii

1 Quine's Conception of Ontology   1
2 Ontology, Language and Existence   16
3 Language, Theory and Belief   32
4 Are there Universals?   42
5 Are there Logical Truths?   72
6 Language and Experience   106

Summary of the Book   123
Notes   128
Bibliography   134
Index   136

Preface

I have never written before on a philosopher or writer with whom I did not feel at least in partial sympathy. This little book is a first exception. What prompted me to write it is the attention and admiration which Quine's work has received when I continue to see little in it. I toyed, at one point, with the idea of calling this book 'The Emperor's Clothes' because that title does really sum up how Quine's philosophical success looks to me from my own little arc. But while I mean to speak my mind I do not wish to imply any disrespect.

I do not mind admitting that as far as symbolic logic goes I cannot hold a candle to Quine. Here, where he is in his element, he quickly leaves me out of my depth. I have, therefore, concentrated on two or three topics he has treated in well known and widely discussed papers : 'On What there is', 'Two Dogmas of Empiricism' (in *From a Logical Point of View*), and 'Epistemology Naturalised' (in *Ontological Relativity and Other Essays*). In these papers I do not have any difficulty in following his arguments and appreciating his intentions. A wider, but by no means complete, familiarity with his work, makes it easier for me to see where he is going in these papers and how his thinking has developed from earlier to later ones. In fact, the different things Quine argues for stand together and give each other mutual support. Whether one wishes to speak of an evolving 'system of thought' here or not, Quine's thought is certainly a well defended fortress. Some central point in his philosophy may strike one as implausible, but the various assumptions on which it rests, perhaps themselves implausible, are explicitly stated and supported in other parts of his work. You cannot easily reject any one thing he asserts without questioning much of the rest of what he says. To be able to construct such a fortress obviously takes ingenuity. Quine is undoubtedly a very clever thinker.

As a philosopher, however, I find him flat and boring. I find his 'mistakes' uninteresting. They do not open up many new questions for me. They give me the feeling 'we have heard it all before', and it amazes me that we should have forgotten it all so quickly. He is and prides himself to be a logician first and foremost, and there is little inconsistency in his work. Unlike that of most great philosophers. But what kind of philosopher lives in this fortress, and what kind of air does he breathe? I find many of the philosophical pronouncements he makes, however many defences he may have for them, immeasurably crude, and the air he breathes stifling. One man's meat, even that of a thousand, may be another man's poison. It may, of course, be my own 'provincialism' that is at fault. However, provided that I treat the aspect of Quine's contribution I discuss with seriousness, and my critical attitude towards it is 'philosophical and not self-assertive' (to use a Socratic expression from the *Phaedo* – 90D) my note of discord need not be offensive. It is certainly not intended to be.

This aspect is indicated in the title of this book. I have obviously isolated these topics from a greater whole which includes Quine's discussions of language and the translatability of different kinds of sentences, and also his discussion of perception and man's contact with the environment in which he lives. These discussions, as I said, very much hang together, although this fact does not make it altogether impossible to treat the topics of my choice on their own and in relative separation from the rest. The negative points for which I argue may be summed up as follows, each one connected with one of the topics indicated in the title of the book in the order in which they appear:

1. Quine's whole notion of ontology is riddled with confusion. In fact 'ontology' is a misnomer for the cluster of philosophical questions the character of which it misrepresents, thus influencing their discussion for ill, not for good.
2. Quine's rejection of the distinction between necessary and contingent truths is unwarranted, and the notion of analyticity in terms of which he conducts this discussion is a red herring.
3. The notion of experience and the subordinate notion of the senses in terms of which Quine discusses the confirmation of propositions and expounds his brand of empiricism are extremely crude. In fact, despite his loud criticism of the logical positivist school of thought Quine remains tied to its apron

strings where it counts most philosophically.

Quine, as I said, is primarily a logician. He believes that the task of philosophy is to construct abstract theories and he, himself, proceeds accordingly. The level of abstraction in which he operates allows his prejudices to take over. His contribution to philosophy is very reminiscent of B.F.Skinner's contribution to psychology. The same spirit informs their writing. Like Skinner, some of the things Quine says are not just crude, but grotesque:

> As illustrated by 'Ouch' (§2), any subjective talk of mental events proceeds necessarily in terms that are acquired and understood through their associations, direct or indirect, with the socially observable behaviour of physical objects. If there is a case for mental events and mental states, it must be just that the positing of them, like the positing of molecules, has some indirect systematic efficacy in the development of theory. But if a certain organisation of theory is achieved by thus positing distinctive mental states and events behind physical behaviour, surely as much organisation could be achieved by positing merely certain correlative physiological states and events instead . . . The bodily states exist anyway; why add the others? Thus introspection may be seen as a witnessing to one's own bodily condition, as introspecting an acid stomach (*Word and Object*, p. 264).

He repeats this, in similar words, in his more recent lectures on 'The Roots of Reference'. What he says about language and how we learn to speak is little better. What amazes me first is that he should be able to say what he says when his references seem to suggest that he is acquainted with recent philosophical discussions on these matters, and secondly that he should be able to get away with it. But then the world we live in is topsy-turvy and has always been so. I intend this as a philosophical remark.

In the book that follows I discuss statements by Quine which I find possible to treat seriously, however wrong-headed I believe them to be.

1 Quine's Conception of Ontology

The first essay in *From a Logical Point of View* is called 'On What there is' (1948). The last chapter of *Word and Object* (1959) is called 'Ontic Decision'. Quine means 'decision about what to admit into our universe'. The same preoccupation runs through the essays published in 1969 together with 'Ontological Relativity' (the lecture given in 1968) under that title. In fact, this question, 'what objects exist?', is one to which Quine keeps returning obsessively.

It is a question which Russell raised in his last lecture in 1918 on 'The Philosophy of Logical Atomism' (1956): 'What is the smallest number of simple undefined things at the start, and the smallest number of undemonstrated premises, out of which you can define the things that need to be defined and prove the things that need to be proved?' Russell believed that this question can only be tackled by means of the apparatus of symbolic logic to the development of which he had made important contributions. In his lectures (1910–11), published under the title *Some Main Problems of Philosophy*, Moore says that one of the most important and interesting things which philosophers have tried to do is no less than give a general description of the *whole* of the universe, mentioning all the most important kinds of thing which we know to be in it (p. 1).

This is the question which Quine discusses in modern clothes. But it never strikes him what a curious question it is. In his paper 'On What there is' he takes himself to be discussing very general *existential* questions, and yet the points he establishes are purely a priori:

1. We *can* use singular terms like 'Pegasus' significantly in sentences *without* presupposing the existence of entities for these

1

terms to name.

2.   We *can* use general terms, for instance the predicate 'red', *without* conceding them to be names for abstract entities.

3.   We *can* view utterances as significant, as synonymous or heteronomous with one another, *without* countenancing a realm of entities called meanings.

In all fairness this is only half of what Quine purports to establish: we do not have to assume the existence of 'possible objects', 'abstract entities' and 'meanings' – not if we don't want to. The question of whether or not we should, Quine would say, is a separate question. With regard to the former question Quine describes himself as having shown 'some common arguments in favour of certain ontologies are fallacious' (p. 19). He describes these as arguments for various forms of Platonism.

One could characterise the points established as 'purely logical' or 'philosophical', except that Quine rejects the contrast on which this characterisation trades – the distinction between what is 'logical' and what is 'empirical', between what is 'philosophical' and what is 'scientific'. I shall return to this question further down. But at least we could, at this stage, restate the three points above differently:

1.   Singular terms like 'Pegasus' do not function as names. The idea that they do comes from certain misunderstandings and leads to certain difficulties.

2.   General terms like 'red' do not function as names either. The idea that they do leads us to misrepresent their relation to the very many occasions on which they are currently used.

3.   The third point becomes a suggestion about how the notion of meaning is to be analysed and how certain difficulties we are liable to meet when we think about it are to be overcome.

When put this way they do not seem to be connected with questions about 'what exists'. But this is not how Quine thinks about them. He sees his arguments as enabling us to escape the compulsion to embrace certain 'ontologies', thus leaving us free to make our own 'ontic decisions'.

He believes these to be responsible to 'pragmatic' considerations and so to be essentially similar to the settling of theoretical questions in the sciences. Thus after having rehearsed the Russellian arguments that we do not have to assume the existence of Pegasus in a possible world in order to speak of its actual non-existence, Quine goes on to indicate reasons for not admitting the existence of 'possible objects' into our universe of discourse: (i) The Platonist's 'over-populated universe is in many ways unlovely. It offends the aesthetic sense of us who have a taste for desert landscapes' (p. 4); (ii) His 'slum of possibles is a breeding ground for disorderly elements' so that the criterion of simplicity alone dictates that we dispense with them (ibid.); (iii) If we tried to treat descriptions that involve contradictions along similar lines we would get into more serious difficulties: 'Unlike Pegasus, the round square cupola on Berkeley College cannot be admitted even as an unactualised *possible*' (p. 5). Quine believes that in the end we have to trim our sails so as to make our journey the most convenient in the prevailing circumstances.

Given, he asks, that we do not have to admit 'possible objects', 'abstract entities', and 'meanings' into our universe, can we avoid *all* ontological commitment? Does whatever we say inevitably commit us to assuming the existence of some entity or other? (p. 12). His answer is that we cannot escape some ontological commitment; necessarily we have to admit some objects into our universe. I wonder what sort of 'necessity' Quine thinks this is?

At any rate his view seems to be this: Necessarily some object or other exists. What objects exist is relative to and, therefore, contingent upon what language we speak. This, in turn, is determined by pragmatic considerations in a way we shall consider further down. But in order to decide what ontological commitment we are to take up and how we are to put it into practice we should be clear about the way we are to assess the ontological commitments that go with a particular language. So Quine distinguishes between two different questions: (i) What are the ontological commitments of a particular language, conceptual scheme or theory? He does not distinguish between these, and overtly repudiates their distinction. Treating them as identical, he advances 'an explicit standard whereby to decide what the ontological commitments of a theory are' (p. 19). (ii) What ontology should we actually adopt? Quine describes his answer to this question as a form of 'pragmatism'. He makes the same distinction at the end of *Word and Object*:

Part of our concern has been with the question what a theory's commitment to objects consist in, and of course this second-order question is about words. But what is noteworthy is that we have talked more of words than of objects even when most concerned to decide what there really is: what objects to admit on our own account (p. 270).

We see that (1) Quine thinks that the use of *any* language whatever commits the speaker to *some* ontology. (2) He thinks that *what* ontology we are committed to depends on the language we speak. (3) He thinks that it is important to devise a method, to advance explicit standards, which will enable us to see clearly the ontological commitments of a particular language. (4) He wants to get clear about the kind of rationale or justification there may be for adopting a particular ontology, for admitting certain objects into our universe.

I have stated Quine's position in his own terms. But none of these terms seems clear to me. What is an 'ontology', and what does Quine mean by a 'language', 'conceptual scheme' or 'theory'? Is it clear that what he has in mind is something we can adopt or reject? I find Quine's views on these questions very dubious for reasons I shall indicate further down. For the moment I shall be content to point out what Quine says and what seems unclear to me.

To begin with what Quine understands by 'ontology' and 'commitment to an ontology'. He says in 'On What there is': 'We commit ourselves to an ontology containing numbers when we say that there are prime numbers larger than a million, we commit ourselves to an ontology containing centaurs when we say there are centaurs; and we commit ourselves to an ontology containing Pegasus when we say Pegasus is. But we do not commit ourselves to an ontology containing Pegasus or the author of *Waverley* or the round square cupola on Berkeley College when we say that Pegasus or the author of *Waverley* or the cupola in question is not' (p. 8). The second and negative part of this statement is clear enough. It says that you can deny the existence of Pegasus or the author of *Waverley* without contradiction. Some philosophers had thought otherwise. Plato was perhaps the first philosopher to discuss this paradox and Russell the first philosopher to resolve it. Quine endorses Russell's solution. But the first part of the above statement is far from clear. If I say that there are prime numbers larger than a million, or that there are three even numbers between 3 and 9, have I committed myself to an ontology containing numbers? If I have, does this mean anything more than 'I have made an arithmetical or numerical statement?' What would it be to opt out of such a commitment?

Is the commitment something implicit in and inseparable from the language or is it the adoption of a 'philosophical theory' regarding the universe of its discourse? Or are the two one and the same thing? Is the question whether the redness of red houses, red roses and red sunsets (Quine's example) something over and above these things an existential question like the question whether Pegasus exists? Surely the question 'What conditions must be satisfied for us to be able to say or think that Pegasus does not exist?' is different from the question whether there ever was a winged horse called Pegasus. Russell and Quine are concerned with the former question and *not* with the latter. If a child, taken in by mythology, says and wrongly believes that the horse Pegasus existed, would he have admitted Pegasus into his ontology? Surely not. Yet this is what Quine claims: 'We commit ourselves to an ontology containing Pegasus when we say Pegasus is.' But if the word 'ontology' means anything at all – and I doubt that it has any coherent meaning[1] – then the 'ontological' claim is that if the word 'Pegasus' means anything there must be something that it names. It is this latter claim that Quine rejects. One can know that Pegasus is only a mythological horse, or wrongly believe that there was a horse called 'Pegasus', without in any way subscribing to the claim which Russell and Quine reject.

Similarly, one can say that there are three even numbers between 3 and 9, without in any way making up one's mind on where one stands on the controversy between Realism and Formalism in the philosophy of mathematics. It is the latter question that Quine is concerned with as a philosopher. Quine denies this: 'The opposition [between Realism and Formalism] is not mere quibble; it makes an essential difference in the amount of classical mathematics to which one is willing to subscribe' (p. 14).

But if it made no such difference, would that make it a 'mere quibble'? Apparently Quine thinks so. Hence his view of the task of philosophy as theory-building and his assimilation of it to the construction of theories in the sciences. Quine continues: 'The sort of ontology we adopt can be consequential – notably in connection with mathematics, although this is only an example' (p. 15). Here Quine speaks of arithmetic and mathematics as at once 'theories', e.g. 'theory of numbers', and 'languages'. I would not object, provided one is clear what it means to talk of a theory in this context. Compare with Professor Toulmin's comparison of theories in physics with maps and languages: The physicist's part in developing a new theory 'is no more than that played by anyone who introduces a language, symbolism, method of representation or system of signs'.[2] But is the 'philosophical theory' of Realism part of classical mathematics in the same way that the classical 'theory of numbers' is part of classical mathematics?

Quine thinks it is so not only here but also in the case of competing philosophical theories about matter: 'Here we have two competing conceptual schemes, a phenomenalistic and a physicalistic one' (p. 17). He then goes on to ask 'Which should prevail?' Unlike Professor Ayer, who in *The Foundations of Empirical Knowledge* spoke of them as 'alternative languages', Quine regards them as similar to conflicting scientific theories: 'Our acceptance of an ontology is, I think, similar in principle to our acceptance of a scientific theory, say a system of physics' (p. 16). He misunderstands what Berkeley meant when he said that 'we ought to think with the learned and speak with the vulgar'.[3] He thinks that insofar as Berkeley speaks with the vulgar he is like the rest of us when 'we speak of the sun as rising'.[4] The implication is that those of us who are educated know that strictly speaking this is false. Thus we differ in our beliefs from those who lived in pre-Copernican times. Similarly, Quine holds, Berkeley differed in his beliefs from his contemporaries. So he calls Berkeley 'a deviant Western intellectual'.[5] But if this is true where does this difference show itself – where in his actions, in his predictions, in his reasonings, in his explanations of everyday phenomena? The difference, in the case of the post-Copernican astronomer, at least shows in the mode of his calculations.

Berkeley, himself, stated plainly that he does not question the existence of things we see with our eyes and touch with our hands.[6] He said that what he was rejecting was 'the philosophic, not the vulgar substance'.[7] He would have denied that these belong to competing conceptual schemes. Locke was, perhaps, inclined to identify his 'philosophic substance' with Newton's invisible, hard and massy particles. But Berkeley certainly did not. He had no wish to reject the scientific findings of his time. No more than Locke. We shall see what rejecting 'the philosophic substance' amounts to, and how it resembles denying that the redness of red houses, roses and sunsets is something over and above these things. In neither case is one denying an existential proposition.

Quine says that 'judged within some particular conceptual scheme . . . an ontological statement goes without saying, standing in need of no separate justification at all' (p. 10). He goes on: 'Ontological statements follow immediately from all manner of casual statements of commonplace fact.' One example he gives is this: 'There is an attribute.' He says that this ontological statement follows from 'There are red houses, red roses, red sunsets.' Another example is: 'There are numbers.' This follows from e.g. 'There are three even numbers between 3 and 9.' But if we speak of attributes and numbers does this make us Platonists? Are we Platonists if we subscribe to the above 'casual statements of commonplace fact' – because they are supposed to commit us to an ontology of attributes and numbers? It is not clear to me where Quine puts the non-philosophical speaker of the English language who constantly subscribes to casual statements of the above kind. As such a speaker am I a Platonist, a Nominalist, or neither? Quine's answer is that I am either a Platonist or a Nominalist depending on whether I think of the claim that red houses, roses and sunsets have something in common as literally true or regard it as merely 'a popular and misleading manner of speaking' (p. 10). But I have no qualms about saying that a rose and a sunset have something in common in that both are red. It is a fact that both are red – provided that they are. So I am a Platonist. On the other hand, I would deny that what makes red things red is something they share, something like the red paint on British telephone booths. So I am a Nominalist. 'Is not this fine reasoning?' – as Hume would say.

What I am asserting in the former case is that both of two red things, a rose and a sunset, are red: a down-to-earth statement of fact unworthy of being dignified as an 'ontology'. What I am rejecting in the latter case is an analogy: the redness of red things is not something over and above them like a coat of paint, something that can exist apart from them as the paint did in the paint box. But to oppose such an analogy is hardly to deny an existential proposition.

We have seen that Quine holds that the use of *any* language whatever commits the speaker to *some* ontology, this ontology varying from one language to another. We can evade a particular ontology by changing our mode of speech: 'When we say that some zoological species are cross-fertile we are committing ourselves to recognising as entities the several species themselves, abstract though they are. We remain so committed at least until we devise some way of so paraphrasing the statement as to show that the seeming reference to species on the part of our bound variable was an avoidable manner of speaking' (p. 13). Unlike Russell he does not regard the paraphrase as providing an analysis of the original statement – one which, as Russell would put it, reveals its 'logical grammar'. Otherwise he would not say that the zoologist's language commits us to an ontology from which the paraphrase frees us. For the paraphrase, on Quine's view, does not give us sentences that are equivalent to those we find in zoology. This is part of Quine's thesis of the relativity of translation with which I am not concerned here. But in that case there is nothing 'seeming' about the reference to zoological species in the language of modern zoology. It is a real reference which the paraphrase is meant to remove. But to what purpose? Ultimately, in the name of a tidier theory. So Quine thinks.

So the paraphrase is a surgical instrument, not an analytical one. But how far can we cut with it? Quine's view is that while we cut in one direction we are grafting new tissue onto our language in another direction – inevitably. He asks: Is there any limit to our ontological immunity? Can we escape it altogether? (p. 12). His answer is that we cannot escape it because every language involves quantification.

Quine argues that it is not names or singular terms that commit us to assuming the existence of something or other, but quantification: 'The use of bound variables is the *only* way we can involve ourselves in ontological commitments. The use of alleged names is no criterion, for we can repudiate their namehood at the drop of a hat unless the assumption of a corresponding entity can be spotted in the things we affirm in terms of bound variables' (ibid.). By repudiating their namehood Quine means converting them into descriptions (e.g. 'Pegasus' = 'the thing that is Pegasus', 'the thing that pegasizes' – see p. 8) and then eliminating the descriptions by means of a Russellian analysis. For as Russell has shown for 'The author of *Waverley* was Scott' to be intelligible, the author of *Waverley* need not exist. It will be remembered that on Russell's analysis the statement in question becomes: 'At least someone wrote *Waverley*, at most someone wrote *Waverley*, and that someone was Scott.'

The existential or 'ontological' presupposition of this statement is the values which 'someone' is meant to take. In other words, one who makes this statement, whether it be true or false, is committed to the affirmation that *men* exist. He cannot assert the above statement and deny that there are men without self-contradiction. This then is how Quine formulates his 'criterion of ontological commitment': 'An entity is presupposed by a theory if and only if it is needed among the values of the bound variables in order to make the statement affirmed in the theory true' (p. 108, and also p. 103). 'A theory is committed to those and only those entities to which the bound variables of the theory must be capable of referring in order that the affirmations made in the theory be true' (pp. 13–14). 'To show that some given object is required in a theory, what we have to show is no more nor less than that the object required, for the truth of the theory, be among the values over which the bound variables range.'[8]

Quine characterises his philosophical position as 'ontological relativism'. For while rival conceptual schemes differ in their ontological presuppositions there is no common measure for objects which a language refers to and so claims to exist without presupposing the whole of that language. So we cannot query such a reference in any absolute sense.[9] We cannot ask which of two rival conceptual schemes mirrors reality more accurately, whether the objects presupposed in a particular language really exist, or exist in reality: 'It is meaningless to inquire into the absolute correctness of a conceptual scheme as a mirror of reality. Our standard for appraising basic changes of conceptual scheme must be, not a realistic standard of correspondence to reality, but a pragmatic standard' (p. 79).

Quine seems to have two different concepts of reality, one differentiated into objects and relative to the language that so differentiates it, and another one which is undifferentiated. This latter is reminiscent of Kant. It is what produces in us 'the disordered fragments of raw experience', the 'scattered sense events': 'Our acceptance of an ontology is, I think, similar in principle to our acceptance of a scientific theory, say a system of physics: we adopt, at least insofar as we are reasonable, the simplest conceptual scheme into which the disordered fragments of raw experience can be fitted or arranged' (p. 16). But for Kant the ordering in question underlies the possibility of applying any empirical concepts and so cannot belong with any form of theoretical consideration. For him experience which is not object-directed 'would be for us as good as nothing' (A.111), 'merely a blind play of representations, less even than a dream' (A.112). Underlying Kant's view is his distinction between the transcendental, a priori and necessary, and the empirical, a posteriori and contingent, which Quine rejects. For Quine all ordering is a matter of theorising: 'A physicalistic conceptual scheme, purporting to talk about external objects, offers great advantages in simplifying our over-all reports. By bringing together scattered sense events and treating them as perceptions of one object, we reduce the complexity of our stream of experience to a manageable conceptual simplicity' (p. 17).

What is unclear to me is what it is that one language, e.g. our 'physicalistic conceptual scheme' is supposed to simplify: the reports made in a different language, e.g. 'phenomenalistic language', or something that goes beyond all language, viz. 'raw experience'? There are difficulties for Quine on either view.

He sometimes speaks as if it is the latter view that he favours. He seems to use such terms as 'raw experience', 'immediate experience', 'individual subjective events of sensation and reflection', 'the complexity of our stream of experience' to refer to something basic or rockbottom which different languages, with their distinctive ontologies, are supposed to 'interpret', 'order', 'organise', 'conceptualise' in their own way. Surely, where it makes sense to speak of ordering there must be something that is ordered, something which can be ordered differently, and presumably something which need not be ordered at all and is in a 'raw' state before the ordering. Kant certainly admitted this when he spoke of 'the raw material of experience'.

Yet this cannot, on Quine's own view, be what a phenomenalistic language enables us to describe, since no language is free of some ontological commitment, and any such commitment entails a form of ordering. This is the other side of Quine. Just as for Kant experience is necessarily object-directed, so for Quine all language necessarily presupposes some ontological commitment: 'Conceptualisation on any considerable scale is inseparable from language.'[10] There is nothing more basic about the ontology of a phenomenalistic language: 'Our ordinary language of physical things is about as basic as language gets.'[11] Hence it is not only physical objects which Quine speaks of as 'posits', but also sense-data: 'No sufficient purpose is served by positing subjective sensory objects.'[12] By 'posit' he means something that is postulated as existing in a particular language and regarded as axiomatic by its speakers. Here Quine remains true to his ontological relativism: 'Viewed from within the phenomenalistic conceptual scheme, the ontologies of physical objects and mathematical objects are myths. The quality of myth, however, is relative; relative, in this case, to the epistemological point of view [of the phenomenalistic conceptual scheme]. This point of view is one among various, corresponding to one among various interests and purposes' (p. 19).

Even at his most relativistic, though, Quine's language reflects the absolutist pull on his thinking: 'Physical objects are postulated entities which round out and simplify our account of the flux of experience.[13] From a phenomenalistic point of view, the conceptual scheme of physical objects is a convenient myth, simpler than the literal truth and yet containing that literal truth as a scattered part' (p. 18). Presumably 'postulate' or 'posit' and 'myth' are not equivalent terms for Quine. Thus physical objects are necessarily 'posits', but they are 'myths' only relative to a phenomenalistic point of view. Yet sometimes Quine uses these terms interchangeably, thereby implying that when we speak of physical objects, numbers and gods we are merely employing conceptual devices to 'expedite our dealings with sense experience' (p. 45), the relative superiority of one over another depending on the efficacy with which they do so: 'The myth of physical objects is epistemologically superior to most in that it has proved more efficacious than other myths as a device for working a manageable structure into the flux of experience' (p. 44).

In the passage just quoted Quine seems to think that any posit must be a myth. But if it does the work for which it has been posited or postulated why should it be a myth? Presumably because it is '*only* a posit'. Only a posit as opposed to what? The question is embarrassing to Quine. Yet he invites it himself when he equates 'posits' and 'myths' when off his guard. I do not think that this is just a slip.

We find that same tension in the contrast between 'the literal truth' and 'a popular and misleading manner of speaking' which Quine would like to regard as relative to the language in which it is made: It is true that red houses, roses and sunsets have something in common, namely redness, but not literally true. It is true only in a 'popular and misleading manner of speaking', relative to a 'formalistic point of view' (see p. 10). It is only with care and vigilance that Quine can suppress the absolutist implications of some of the expressions that come to his pen naturally.

In short, if the reality to which the phenomenalistic conceptual scheme commits us is 'raw', as Quine describes it, and therefore 'unconceptualised', then we have here an ontology which is *not* relative to a particular language. If, on the other hand, Quine thinks of the idea of an absolute ontology as confused, then what does he mean by 'raw'? I don't think that Quine has resolved this dilemma. Behind his sophisticated relativism, with which I have some sympathy, there lurks a primitive absolutism which he tries to disown, not altogether successfully. We shall understand better in the later part of this book the reasons for his failure; they are rooted in the very form of empiricism which he embraces.

Despite this tension, however, Quine holds that one's ontology is relative to the language one speaks, and that there is no question of stepping outside language altogether. In that case, how is one supposed to decide what there is? Quine says: There is no 'vantage point outside the conceptual scheme that he [the philosopher] takes in charge . . . He cannot study and revise the fundamental conceptual scheme of science and common sense without having some conceptual scheme, whether the same or another no less in need of philosophical scrutiny, in which to work. He can scrutinise and improve the system from within.'[14] He is, Quine says, using a simile from Neurath, like a captain who has to rebuild his boat at sea, plank by plank, without putting ashore. Each time he changes a plank the rest of the planks keep him afloat. Yet by the time he has gone through each plank, one by one, the boat is made entirely of new planks; there is not one old plank which has not been changed. What can be done with the boat, Quine argues, can be done with language.

Deciding what there is, in this sense, *is* deciding what language to use. It is, for instance, deciding how best to go on developing mathematics: Shall we accept irrational numbers, infinite numbers? It is, to give another example, deciding how best to organise the experimental data in a particular science: How shall we interpret the results of the experiments devised by Priestley and Lavoisier? Shall we speak of the loss of phlogiston or the gain of oxygen?[15] But although it is a question of deciding what language to use, it is not a linguistic question: 'I am not suggesting (Quine says) a dependence of being upon language . . . What there is does not in general depend on one's use of language, but what one says there is does' (p. 103).

In what sense does Quine think that this question of 'what there is' depends on language? He says that although 'ontological controversy . . . tends into controversy over language . . . we must not jump to the conclusion that what there is depends on words' (p. 16). He continues: 'Our acceptance of an ontology is, I think, similar in principle to our acceptance of a scientific theory, say a system of physics.' He thinks of a theory as a symbolism which organises the data obtained by observation and experiment, and he envisages the possibility of different ways of organising this data. He thinks, I suspect, in a way that is reminiscent of Wittgenstein in the *Tractatus*, that the fact that a particular symbolism or theory organises the data in question in a more economical and convenient way than a different symbolism or theory depends on how things stand – and this is not a matter of language.[16]

Wittgenstein's account, however, unlike Quine's, is meant to apply to mechanics, which may be regarded as the geometry of physics, and not to language as such. Wittgenstein, unlike Quine, distinguishes been scientific truths and truths of logic: 'And now we can see the relative position of logic and mechanics' (6.342). Later he would have said that there are limits to what the speakers of a language can question in the way Quine has in mind. This is the question of the 'inexorability' of logic which Wittgenstein, as we shall see, treats very differently from Quine.

To sum up Quine's view on this question: 'How are we to adjudicate among rival ontologies?' (p. 15). One's ontology is internal and, therefore, relative to the language one uses. But there is still the question whether this language is the one *best suited* to the purposes of one's researches and inquiries. To accept an ontology is to adopt a language or conceptual scheme, and one's reasons for doing so are extra-linguistic. Since they are bound up with one's practical purposes Quine characterises them as 'pragmatic'.

In the following three chapters my main criticism of Quine will be that what he calls 'ontology' has nothing to do with existence. To quote Quine's words again: 'Physical objects are postulated entities which round out and simplify our account of the flux of experience, just as the introduction of irrational numbers simplifies laws of arithmetic' (p. 18). I have no objection to speaking of the 'introduction' of irrational numbers into mathematics and claiming that doing so 'simplifies laws of arithmetic'. But this is the introduction of a conceptual device, a momentous one, and has nothing to do with existence – as I hope to argue later. Further, laws of arithmetic, thus simplified, are not an account of anything. What is true is that they are used in accounts which physicists give of the various phenomena they study. It is true, also, that they enable physicists to provide simpler accounts of these than they otherwise might have done. However, these are accounts of such phenomena as electricity, heat, light, and so on. They are not accounts of 'the flux of experience'.

This is where we shall find one of the big differences between Quine and Wittgenstein. The latter says: 'Concepts help us to comprehend things. They correspond to a particular way of dealing with situations.'[17] There is no mention of experience here as in Quine's writings where the term 'experience' trades on our everyday use of this term but does not have an intelligible sense. The words 'things' and 'situations' which Wittgenstein uses, on the other hand, are meant to refer to what we face in our lives as language users. What the users of different languages face may, to a greater or lesser extent, vary with the language they use and the culture to which the language belongs. But there is no suggestion in Wittgenstein of an underlying identity as is implied by Quine's notion of 'raw experience' or 'the flux of experience'. The tension in Quine comes from the conflict between his 'empiricism' and his 'relativism' which are irreconcilable.

My second and more immediate criticism is connected with something I said earlier, namely that there is a tension in Quine between wanting to equate existential claims with the postulation of entities and feeling that such postulation somehow falls short of what we mean by existence – a feeling that finds expression in his characterisation of all such posits as 'myths'. If he were able to accept the distinction Wittgenstein makes between 'logical concepts' and 'ordinary concepts' or 'concepts proper' and acknowledge that it is only in connection with the latter that we talk of existence in the ordinary sense the tension would be resolved. But since he explicitly rejects the distinction between logical and empirical truth he cannot recognise any difference between the philosopher's 'There are no physical objects' or its denial and the ordinary negative existential claim 'There are no unicorns' or its denial.

As I said before, in Quine everything is connected and one cannot bring any one part of what he holds into question without doing so for the rest. To reject what he says one has to pull down the whole zip. In what follows I intend to do so only part of the way.

2 Ontology, Language and Existence

In the title page of *Word and Object* Quine quotes an epigram from James Grier Miller: 'Ontology recapitulates philology', obviously fashioned after the well-known epigram, 'Ontology recapitulates philogeny', meaning that the development of the individual reduplicates the development of the species. Likewise, Quine believes, our views regarding what exists in nature, or 'the ultimate furniture of the world' as Russell once put it, evolve with the language that we speak. It is Quine's view that this evolution of which 'ontology' and 'philology' are the two aspects, like the two sides of a coin, is subject to investigation and, therefore, responsive to reason. He holds, as we have seen, that since our ontology is internal to the language we speak and since we cannot step outside language altogether, we can only appraise our ontology in a piece-meal way, as Neurath's captain renewed his ship plank by plank without putting ashore.

Accordingly, in the last chapter of *Word and Object*, Quine undertakes this piece-meal task. He discusses the questions: Are there physical objects, sense-data, propositions, classes, attributes, measures (e.g. miles, degrees Fahrenheit), possible objects, facts, infinitesimals (e.g. instantaneous velocities), ideal objects (e.g. mass points, frictionless surfaces), geometrical objects, ordered pairs, numbers, minds? The list is indeed peculiar to 'ontology'. But what does someone who asks whether any of these things exist wish to know?

Take two of the extreme items in Quine's list which he only mentions in passing: 'sakes' and 'behalves'. Nobody, not even a philosopher, asks seriously whether there are 'sakes' and 'behalves', or whether the word 'sake' in the sentence 'Please, do it for my sake' names or stands for an entity. This, however, is not true of 'and' and 'not'. Thus Russell at one time thought that

16

such logical connectives are objects. We know how Wittgenstein dealt with this claim in the *Tractatus* and what alternative account he put in its place. But are we to say that Wittgenstein was reducing the ontology he had inherited from Russell? If he thought that Russell was wrong, as he did, how did he think Russell was wrong? What sort of misapprehension was he under? Is it really like the misapprehension of the child who, steeped in mythology, believes that there are fire-breathing dragons?

Quine's answer is a considered, deliberate Yes. His view, if I understand it rightly, is this: To claim that there are dragons is to claim something false or untrue in the sense that we cannot keep this statement without making many adjustments to what else we wish to say on a thousand different occasions. To keep it is not worth the inconvenience of these adjustments. This is what is meant by claiming it to be false. It is because the child obviously goes along with the rest of us in his linguistic responses everywhere else that he is wrong when he believes that there are fire-breathing dragons. It is the same, Quine tells us, with his fictitious philosopher Wyman who believes in the existence of the possible fat man standing at the door. When he is shown what it would cost him to keep this statement and others like it, he will have the choice of paying the price or retracting what he now claims. Quine thinks that unless he is utterly perverse, those considerations of convenience, economy, etc., that weigh with us will equally weigh with him and persuade him to retract his claim and thus reduce his ontology.

While I think that it is indeed the case that when we assert a statement, consider or affirm its truth, we take for granted, and are ready to go along with, much else that belongs to speaking the language in which the statement is made, I do not think that Quine's account does justice to either the example of the child or that of the philosopher. Nor, therefore, does it succeed in papering over the differences between them. The child has simply come to believe what he was told or what he read because he mistook the way it was intended. He could have come to the same belief by believing a lie. The philosopher Wyman, on the other hand, is in the grip of a puzzle or paradox and he suggests a way of resolving it. This involves regarding what does not exist, Pegasus, as something that exists in the realm of possibility. But what does regarding it as such come to or involve? Is this a belief? Is it like believing that there is a distant land where are to be found fire-breathing dragons and winged horses, even when they cannot be seen or touched? Is this really what Plato meant by 'purely intelligible objects'?

Wittgenstein remarked that 'when we do philosophy we are like savages'.[1] In a short contribution to a BBC symposium, *The Physical Basis of Mind*, Professor Ryle compared the Cartesian philosopher to peasants in a story who were terrified at the sight of their first railway train and were not pacified by their parson's explanation of how a steam engine works. They thought there must be an angry horse inside the locomotive. When they examined it and could find no horse there, they insisted that there was nevertheless a ghost-horse there which, like fairies, is invisible to mortal eyes. Ryle's story goes: 'The pastor objected, "But, after all, horses themselves are made of moving parts, just as the steam-engine is made of moving parts. You know what their muscles, joints and blood-vessels do. So why is there a mystery in the self-propulsion of a steam-engine, if there is none in that of a horse? What do you think makes the horse's hooves go to and fro?" After a pause a peasant replied, "What makes the horse's hooves go is four extra little ghost-horses inside." ' Ryle comments that 'just such a story has been the official theory of the mind for the last three very scientific centuries'.[2]

This comparison between the philosopher and savages is misleading, as both Wittgenstein and Ryle would acknowledge.[3] Even Quine is not altogether happy with it and contrasts the philosophical immaterialist, whom he misleadingly describes as a 'deviant Western intellectual', with someone who belongs to a different culture and holds some different beliefs from us. Certainly someone who may be described as subscribing to the Cartesian view of the mind does not hold any *beliefs* different from us, nor does he differ from us in his everyday judgements and reasonings about people. His difference, not so much from us as from the Behaviourist philosopher, will appear in his verbal responses to philosophical questions. But since these words are not connected with his expectations, and most of his other words and reasonings, in the way that the same words in the mouth of Ryle's peasants may be, we cannot say that they mean the same or express the beliefs which Ryle imagines to have animated his peasants.

The peasants may not expect to see a horse inside the engine, nor even to hear it. Perhaps some of them believe that if they spend the night in a railway yard they might hear and even see the horse, ethereal against the dark of the night. But even if they did not believe this, they might still be reluctant to spend the night there for fear of the influence this may have on the course of their lives. This fear would be surrounded with certain thoughts. Certainly their attitude towards the locomotive will be very different from ours; they will think of it in different terms, and the thought and sight of it will evoke different feelings in them. We could express the difference in terms of existential beliefs which separate us, say that they believe in the existence of an invisible horse which moves the locomotive (or what *we* call 'locomotive') along the track. Compare with our belief in colourless, odourless and tasteless gases and consider what the content of this belief comes to in terms of our expectations and experimental procedures. In contrast the Behaviourist and Cartesian philosophers are separated in none of the ways in which Ryle's imaginary peasants and members of Western contemporary society are separated in their behaviour, attitudes, feelings and expectations concerning railway engines. In his introduction to *The Concept of Mind* Ryle himself states explicitly that what he polemically characterises as a myth and combats is not 'a fairy story'. He says that 'to explode a myth is not to deny the facts but to re-allocate them'.[4]

Quine rejects this contrast between stating or denying facts and re-allocating them, doing so because he is wedded to a philosophical theory which I shall examine later. But the point in question was once made by characterising the positive and negative claims made by philosophers as 'idle' or 'empty hypotheses'. This was meant to emphasise the fact that they are not directed to altering our expectations and behaviour, or intended to explain any phenomena. True, some philosophers may think or half-think that they were advancing existential hypotheses, positive or negative. Thus McTaggart: 'So matter is in the same position as the gorgons and the harpies.' But, surely, how anyone means his words and what it is he believes is to be seen in what else he says, what he does and expects on a thousand different occasions. It is precisely this lack of connection between the pronouncements in question and the philosopher's words and actions elsewhere that has puzzled Hume and also Moore. Moore found it 'strange' that 'philosophers should have been able to hold sincerely, as part of their philosophical creed, propositions inconsistent with what they themselves *knew* to be true'.[5] He found it 'curious' that a philosopher could be sceptical about certain sorts of things without being '*in doubt* about anything whatever'.[6]

This strangeness, which comes from misunderstanding, shifts place if we say that the claims in question are 'empty', that they are idle wheels that do not move any other part of the mechanism of communication. This was the response of positivist, verificationist philosophers. However we should still find it 'strange' that philosophers who made the claims in question should not have realised that their words were 'empty'. Where Moore was puzzled by the inconsistency of the philosophers in question, what the positivists say about them leave us puzzled by their muddle-headedness.

The next move comes with the realisation that what these philosophers were advancing were not idle or empty hypotheses, for they were not hypotheses at all. Thus Wisdom: 'The statements: "Matter doesn't exist", "Matter doesn't really exist", "Matter isn't anything over and above our sensations", "Matter is a logical fiction", "Statements about material things can be analysed into statements about sensations" form a series.'[7] Note that Wisdom is not saying that they are equivalent. He would say that the question whether they are equivalent or not is a 'conflict question' – like the question whether a tomato is a fruit or a vegetable, or the question in his example, adapted from William James, whether the dog which circles around the place where a cow stands without succeeding in getting past its horns circles around the cow. Wisdom says: 'As the formulations become more and more logical and analytical and less scientific and like hypotheses, something is gained and something is lost.'[8]

The loss Wisdom has in mind, very briefly, is the loss of the sense of wonder in philosophy. The loss of the sense that the philosopher is someone who struggles with 'illusion, delusion and misapprehension', even if not of the kind which these were first thought to be. It gives place to the view that the philosopher is a kind of logical cartographer concerned with accuracy and precision. What is more, on this view, he is thought of as studying not the plains and cities in which we live and walk about, but their maps. The gain in moving towards such a conception consists in the fact that in doing so we cease to think of the philosopher as a kind of master-scientist who is concerned to investigate the most general and abstract features of the world, doing so what is more without leaving his ivory tower. Quine rejects this contrast between logic and science as spurious, but he retains the worst of both worlds in his philosophy. His conception of philosophy, it seems to me, combines the worst features of the two views of philosophy which Wisdom contrasts.

In contrast with Moore and McTaggart, Wisdom claims that the philosopher who says that Matter doesn't exist, contrary to appearances, is really advancing a 'simile for the logic of matter'.[9] Is this not sufficiently clear in the case of Berkeley? 'I do not argue against the existence of any one thing that we can apprehend, either by sense or reflection. That the things I see with mine eyes and touch with my hands do exist, really exist, I make not the least question.'[10]

Quine may reply: 'Perhaps not. But he was still denying the existence of something, namely a substratum which supports the sensible qualities of material things and explains their co-existence in clusters. His conflict may not be with us, the vulgar, with common sense, but with Locke. His ontology perhaps coincides with that of common sense, but it certainly does not with Locke's ontology.' But the same question could be raised about Locke – or any other philosopher who claims that material things are something over and above the sense-impressions from which we know them and on which we base what we say about them: Is he saying that besides the table that we see and touch there is another table which we cannot see and touch, 'an unknown somewhat', or is he saying that the table that we see and touch does not stop existing when we no longer see it and touch it? If he is saying the latter, then surely Locke, no more than Berkeley, is putting forward an existential claim. He, no more than Berkeley, is in conflict with us – with common sense. The claim that the conflict between these two philosophers is a conflict in ontology is by now beginning to wear thin.

In 'Existence and Quantification' Quine admits that he 'has been playing down the difference between common sense existence statements, as of rabbits and unicorns, and philosophical existence statements, as of numbers and attributes'.[11] He says that there is also a curious difference between them that needs to be played up. A philosophical theory such as that of Berkeley in *Principles of Human Knowledge*, or better that of Carnap in *Logical Structure of the World*, 'might accommodate all rabbit data and yet admit as values of its variables no rabbits or other bodies, but only qualities, time and places. The adherents of that theory . . . would have a sentence which, as a whole, had the same stimulus meaning as our sentence ''There is a rabbit in the yard''; yet in the quantificational sense of the words they would have to deny that there is a rabbit in the yard or anywhere else.''[12] In other words, an adherent to such a theory would use a particular sentence S on every occasion when we would say 'There is a rabbit in the yard'. Given that there is a similar correspondence between all his other sentences and ours, surely his sentence S and our sentence 'There is a rabbit in the yard' would by synonymous. So I would say: Too bad for 'the quantificational sense of his words'. The equivalence may, of course, be only apparent. This would be the case where there are divergencies between other parts of the language in which S is used and our language, and between our respective lives and activities. But this is precisely what is not the case with the adherent of a philosophical theory, as in the case of Berkeley and Carnap.

Berkeley was happy to continue to speak the language of the vulgar – as long, he said, as we are prepared to think with the learned. Carnap, it is true, went on to construct a language for the learned. This is a step towards the kind of formalism we find in Quine where what we mean is dictated by the possibilities of the logician's canonical notation – in this case what a particular philosopher means. Thus Quine tries to force Ayer and Ryle into the mould of his canonical notation of quantification, despite their protest: 'You say ''There are concepts with which . .'', ''. . . some of which propositions . . .'', ''. . . there is something that he doubts or believes'', you cannot therefore blandly disavow any claim that there are such objects as concepts and propositions. You are committed to an ontology of such objects unless you retract your words, rewrite your philosophy.'[13] Quine wishes Ayer and Ryle to follow Carnap, and just as he constructed a language which does not mention or refer to rabbits and the like, to write their philosophy in a language that does not mention propositions and concepts, or else to face the music. He says: 'To decline to explain oneself in terms of quantification . . . is simply to decline to disclose one's referential intent.'[14]

We have two questions here: (i) Does Carnap deny the existence of rabbits? Is he committed to doing so? (ii) Are Ayer and Ryle committed to affirming the existence of propositions? As I said, surely Carnap thinks in terms of our language and lives the life of that language. The language he has constructed is neither an alternative nor a substitute for the language he speaks. I put it in terms of the language which Carnap speaks (or spoke) and not in terms of the ontology he accepts and of whether this includes rabbits and the like. I find the whole of this latter notion suspect: Does he accept or deny the existence of rabbits? Does he not, like Berkeley, think that there are rabbits 'in the yard or anywhere else'? Would he not say that there are if asked?

It is these questions that I find suspect. Do we think that there are rabbits? Do I? Just like that I wouldn't know what to say because I do not know what is being asked. 'Are there rabbits in Australia?' I understand this question. But it has nothing to do with ontology, if by that we are to understand an inquiry in which such questions as 'Are there material things?' are discussed. Despite Quine's arguments I do not see that the claim that there are rabbits in Australia is continuously related to the philosopher's existential assertions. Behind the claim that they are so related lies the unspoken presupposition that language, or the sentences of language, serve always one and the same purpose, namely to state or describe something. Indeed, it entirely ignores the multiplicity of concerns and interests that find expression in the uses of language. This is, at least in part, responsible for Quine's assimilation of philosophical questions to scientific ones. Instead of *looking* at what philosophers who ask existential questions are engaged in and considering what their difficulties are, he *legislates* about what they must be doing. He is too much attached to his theory, given the many layered defenses which he has constructed around it with great ingenuity, to be able to take a disinterested view of the matter.

To return to our rabbits. Given the right kind of story, I can imagine a sense for 'Are there rabbits?', asked as one may ask 'Are there dinosaurs?', or even 'Are there unicorns?'. But, again, these questions have little to do with the philosopher's existential questions which do not limit themselves to rabbits, nor to any particular place or time. It is the lifting of these restrictions that makes a radical difference to the identity of his questions. It changes them from existential to conceptual questions. But this needs explaining.

All right, the philosopher's existential question is not confined to rabbits, nor is it limited to any particular place, say Australia, or time, say since the great myxomatosis that spread across all the continents. How is this 'absolute generality' to be expressed and understood? 'Rabbits *and the like* do not exist.' The natural response would be: Do you mean the whole species? Or do you mean something wider: all mammals? all animals? all living things? all organic matter? You can't be serious! We have wider and wider classes with their special defining characteristics or distinguishing features. Here we are in the realm of what we use language to identify, classify, distinguish, refer to, describe. We could say that 'rabbits, mammals, vertebrates, animals, living things, organic matter . . .' form a series. The question is whether 'physical object' belong to this series.

Let us say, with Quine, that the philosopher is wondering whether physical objects exist anywhere and at any time. But even the expressions 'anywhere' and 'any time' usually presuppose a dimension or space within which, if a question is asked, the searching is to proceed: 'Has gold been discovered *anywhere* on this continent, or in this country, at *any time* in the history of its republic?' 'Nowhere' needs completion: 'Nowhere in this room', 'nowhere on this planet'. If this is not explicitly mentioned, it is certainly understood in the particular context in which the word is used in discourse. Similarly for 'at no time': 'At no time in the history of mankind.' Without these restrictions the philosopher's existential question or statement becomes a-spatial and a-temporal. It turns away from the contingent to the possible and intelligible. Thus 'Are there physical objects?' can be reformulated into 'Can there be? Can we make sense of the existence of physical objects? Is the notion itself intelligible? Does it not hide a contradiction?'. Berkeley explicitly reformulated his claim that 'Matter doesn't exist' into 'Matter is nothing but ideas', and he reformulated that, in turn, into 'The conception of matter, as something distinct from our ideas, hides a contradiction'. So his question was not really concerned with the existence of anything, but with what it *means* to claim that material things exist independently of being perceived. Berkeley, like the rest of us, knew well enough what this means, but the more he thought about it the more difficult he found to make coherent sense of this notion. He described well the plight of the philosopher in his Introduction when he said: 'No sooner do we meditate on the nature of things [i.e. the distinction between matter and ideas, the way the former but not the latter exists in-dependently of being perceived] but a thousand scruples spring up in our minds, concerning those things which before we seemed fully to comprehend. Prejudices do from all parts discover themselves to our view; and endeavouring to correct these by reason, we are insensibly drawn into uncouth paradoxes, dif-ficulties, and inconsistencies, which multiply and grow upon us as we advance in speculation.' This is precisely what Wisdom means when he describes philosophy as a struggle with 'illusion, delusion and misapprehension' and complains that it is lost in the idea and practice of philosophy as 'logical geography'.

So it turns out that ordinary existential questions, such as whether there are kangaroos in America or rabbits in Antarctica, have nothing to do with ontology. They are radically different from the philosopher's existential questions. On the other hand, the philosopher's existential questions are not really existential questions at all. So we can say that there is no such thing as on-tology, meaning that the idea of the philosopher as concerned with 'what there is' comes from confusion. Wisdom used to say that ontological questions are really epistemological questions in disguise. He meant that when philosophers ask whether, for in-stance, there are physical objects, they are questioning whether physical objects are anything over and above the sense impres-sions from which alone, it seems, we can know their existence, i.e. know the truth of such propositions as 'There is cheese in the larder'. He said that 'Matter doesn't exist' is in many ways like 'The average man doesn't exist'. The latter statement forcibly combats something which ordinary language suggests, namely that the average man is related to the individual men whose tastes, habits and earnings he represents in the way that a member of Parliament is related to his constituency.[15] It is clear that what this latter statement combats is a logical or conceptual misapprehension. What Wisdom offers is a comparison to bring out the extent to which this is equally true of the philosopher's 'Matter doesn't exist'.

We have already seen how much this is true of Berkeley. For having denied the existence of matter Berkeley went on to point out that what he was concerned to combat was a conception of matter such as we find in Locke. He was concerned to do so because of the sceptical consequences of Locke's conception. For if one holds that matter is something over and above the sense impressions from which alone we can know the truth of ordinary existential statements about cheese in the larder and rabbits in Australia, one cannot escape the conclusion that our sense impressions give us at best inductive grounds for such statements. But once we accept this, we cannot avoid the further conclusion that we cannot know anything about physical objects, that for all we know the whole of life may be a dream. Once we see that this is what Berkeley was concerned to combat, we shall see the justice in Wisdom's claim that his existential denial is directed to epistemological issues and arises out of epistemological preoccupations – in short, that ontological questions are really epistemological questions in disguise.

Quine may retort: 'Surely, what Berkeley opposes is the postulation of an entity, a substratum or support for the sensible qualities of material things. He denies that such an entity exists. The controversy, therefore, is over ontology. The question he is discussing is whether we need to postulate such an entity to explain the recurrent patterns of our sense experience. This is in no way different from the scientific postulation of theoretical entities to explain certain experimental results.' Quine's view is that our concept of physical object is a postulate the aim of which is to 'reduce the complexity of our stream of experience to a manageable simplicity' (p. 17). He speaks of the concept of physical object as belonging to a 'physicalistic conceptual scheme', and sometimes to that of 'common sense'.

Now a theory is something that we construct or develop when certain phenomena puzzle us. They raise certain questions for us which we pursue, and it is this pursuit that finally leads to the theory in which we answer at least some of these questions. To ask such questions we must already have a place on which to stand, and we acquire such a place in learning to speak. This learning to speak involves learning to act and acquiring various concepts. Among other things, very early in life, the young child learns e.g. to follow his rattle with his eyes, to reach for it, to hold it, to put it into his mouth, to look for it when it is put away outside his line of vision, etc. Acquiring these elementary reactions or modes of behaviour *is* an important part of what we may describe as his coming to possess the concept of a physical object or of physical reality. Neither then nor later does it make sense to explain or justify such reactions: Why do you look for the rattle which you want to have when you can no longer see it? Because it is a physical object and physical objects have a continued existence. No, a physical object is just the kind of thing to which it makes sense to behave in this way. 'It is because it is a physical object, and because physical objects have continued existence that we respond in these ways': This is putting the cart before the horse.

What is it to think that what you see is a physical object and not an hallucination? It is not because it is a physical object that you will continue to see it later. Rather if you do see later what you see now you will say that what you see is a physical object. This is part of what we mean by 'physical object', and neither is it something that we *find out* about physical objects – e.g. find out that they have continued existence.[16] The point I am getting at is this: The concept of physical object, like some others, e.g. number, colour, quality, etc., are not ordinary concepts, and they are taken for granted in our theorisings. To possess such a concept is to possess familiarity with certain customs, the ability to enter into and go on with certain practices and activities. To possess the concept of number, for instance, is being able to count, add, divide, etc. These are fundamental in the sense that they underlie the possibility of putting forward hypotheses, giving explanations, and even asking questions, including existential ones. Therefore these concepts themselves cannot be characterised as theoretical concepts or postulates – as Quine does.

In these concepts we are not dealing with *existence* at all, but with *forms* of language, thought and apprehension. Take the concept of unicorn which is an ordinary concept – an example I have used before.[17] One may possess this concept, know what a unicorn is, and still not know whether or not there are unicorns – just as one who understands the meaning of an ordinary empirical proposition need not know whether or not it is true. In contrast a person who may be described as possessing the concept of material thing is one who is familiar with the use of a whole host of words, such as 'rabbit', 'table', 'hand', 'ashtray', etc., and that means he recognises the *possibility* of saying true things with these words.

But is this a question of what exists? Someone may say: 'Unless there were such things as rabbits, tables, sticks, stones, and the like, it would not be possible to say true things with the words in question.' He would be suggesting that the possibility of truth and, therefore, of sense depends on what actually exists. Obviously, if there were no such animals as rabbits you could not say anything true with the word 'rabbit' – except that rabbits do not exist and what they would be like if they existed. Just as you cannot truthfully say that unicorns are grazing in yonder field. But when we say that what this sentence says is false we are speaking in the language of physical objects. Any one or more things we say in that language may be false, but there must be some things we could say that would be true. A language in which we could never say what is true is no language at all. Where there is language there must be the possibility of truth. But if we were to say 'There are no such things as rabbits and the like', meaning 'and the like' in the way in which Moore tried to mean it, we would be using the very language which we are trying to base on the truth of what we are trying to say. This would be going round in a circle.

I said that where there is language there must be the possibility of truth. That is there must be the possibility of using the words in its vocabulary and their combinations in properly constructed sentences to say what is true. We could say that the language guarantees the possibility of saying something true with its sentences, and that means true by standards of truth internal to the language. The language of physical objects is, of course, the whole of language insofar as reference to physical objects goes through the whole of language. This language itself guarantees that *some* statements made in it will be true – statements in which we refer to rabbits 'and the like', which in short philosophers have referred to as physical objects. Obviously, language is silent about *which* of its possible statements are true. That depends on extra-linguistic facts, though we cannot think of them without the language in question.

If language is necessarily silent about *which* statements intelligible in that language are true, neither can it tell us what exists. In the *Tractatus* Wittgenstein said that it cannot tell us *what* exists, but that it presupposes that something or other exists (see 5.552). But 'something or other exists' says no more than 'some existential statements in the language will be true'. In other words, the language in question provides for the possibility or intelligibility of existential statements – such statements as 'There is cheese in the larder', 'There are cows grazing in the field'. This says no more than that statements of this form make sense and, therefore, can be true. In other words, what a language guarantees is the intelligibility of statements made in that language, including existential statements made in it; and that means guarantees the possibility of their truth. But to say that certain forms of existential statements can be true is not to say what exists, i.e. it is not to make an existential statement. To say that propositions of a certain form can be true is not to say that any proposition is true, i.e. it is not to utter any truth about what we use language to talk about.

If one were to say 'Physical objects exist' one would be saying no more than 'Physical object propositions, including existential physical object propositions like "There is cheese in the larder", make sense and, therefore, can be true.' This makes it clear that it is not an existential statement – contrary to appearances. But this is not what philosophers who use these words wish to say.

Quine subscribes to the statement that 'Ontology recapitulates philology.' But it turns out that this is not the exciting statement he cracks it up to be, since ontology turns out to have nothing to do with existence. We could rephrase it as 'Philology recapitulates philology' which is a tautology and says nothing.

The concept of physical object – this is not a concept in the language. To acquire it is to learn the language. What the concept or the language guarantees is the intelligibility of certain statements, including certain existential statements, and that means the possibility of their truth. So Wittgenstein says: 'One might say of logical concepts that their essence proves their existence.'[18] All this means is that the intelligibility of a logical concept, e.g. physical object, guarantees the possibility of saying true things with physical object words. To possess this concept *is* to recognise that it is possible to say true things with physical object words, which one might describe as 'recognising the existence of physical objects'. Compare with: 'To understand a logical proposition means recognising its truth.'

The platitude that there are physical objects, or that physical objects exist, is thus not an existential statement at all. It is an unreflective expression of allegiance to the language one speaks in the face of what one takes to be a challenge. It is like stamping one's feet as if to indicate where one stands. But this is a pretty futile gesture[19] – in contrast with for example a theist's affirmation that 'God exists', which is another way of saying 'I believe in God'. But is that an existential statement? I am not saying that it is not; I am merely asking. Quine says: 'Physical objects are . . . irreducible posits comparable, epistemologically, to the gods of Homer. For my part I do, *qua* lay physicist, believe in physical objects and not in Homer's gods; and I consider it a scientific error to believe otherwise' (p. 44). Quine is wrong both about physical objects, as I have argued, and about Homer's gods. He is immeasurably crude in his few scattered remarks about the latter, in fact a complete philistine. But I am not now concerned with this.

I referred to the statement 'There are physical objects' as a platitude. But it is no ordinary platitude. It is, I said, an unreflective expression of allegiance to the language one speaks in the face of what one takes to be a challenge. If there is a challenge, however, it is not language that is being challenged, and what one defends in the face of it is not the language one speaks. I doubt that that can be challenged and, therefore, that it needs a defence.[20] There is a challenge in the question 'Are there physical objects?', but to understand it one has to consider the philosophical difficulties from which the question comes. What the challenge is will become plain only after the question has been transformed several times through the different stages of its discussion. Quine never asks what these difficulties might be.

Certainly what is in question is *not*, as Quine thinks, whether we can do without the concept of physical object, in the way in which the question whether there are atoms, at least as asked by physicists at one time, was partly – but only partly – a question of whether physics would be better off without the atomic theory of matter.[21] Carnap may have thought so in *The Logical Structure of the World*. But if one puts his discussion in the wider context to which it belongs one cannot say that even Carnap thought so without qualification. Was he trying to construct a language to replace the language in which we speak of rabbits, sticks and stones? I mean in the various practical situations in which we use this language? I think that the answer is No, and that he thought that the utility of his artificial language does not lie in its practical service to us, but in its capacity to show us something about the natural language which serves us very well. That is I take it that Carnap, like Berkeley, would be happy to speak with the vulgar, and that his artificial language was his way of thinking with the learned. This brings his venture into the mainstream of philosophical discussion on which I have commented and which Quine badly misrepresents.

As for the second question I mentioned above: Are there propositions? Are Ayer and Ryle committed to affirming the existence of propositions? This needs a somewhat different treatment. Part of what is being asked, but only part of it, is whether as philosophers discussing certain questions about language, logic and knowledge it would be a help or a hindrance to frame and discuss these questions in a language that mentions propositions: Does doing so bring in philosophical pre-suppositions which are objectionable? I do not propose to discuss this question; but I do not think that it is an existential question: 'Are there such entities as propositions?' Nor is the question one that is concerned with the merits and demerits of a theory.

3 Language, Theory and Belief

Quine, we have seen, holds that each language commits the speaker to a particular ontology. He also thinks that language is something to which we subscribe, even if not consciously and deliberately. We can become conscious of it and subject our commitments to questioning and criticism. To do so is to engage in philosophy. As something to which we subscribe Quine thinks of language as a theory, one which helps us to interpret and organise what he calls 'the stream of experience' or 'raw experience'.

I have argued that Quine's notion of ontology is badly confused, and I contrasted language to a theory. I shall return to his notion of 'raw experience' which I shall argue is incoherent. At present I want to ask (1) whether the language we speak does commit us to anything, and if so to what, (2) whether we do really have any choice in what language we speak, and where pragmatic considerations enter the evolution of any language, and (3) whether language can be characterised as a theory, and whether a scientific theory can be characterised as a particular kind of language. Questions (1) and (3) are closely connected and I shall take them together.

The idea that the language we speak commits us to anything conjures up the image of assenting to a proposition and then finding that one is committed to assenting to a further proposition that follows from the first one. But inferences are what we make, conclusions are what we draw, *in* the speaking of language. And what is in question is whether we are committed to anything as part of speaking a particular language. If we speak a language then, presumably, we hope to communicate with others who speak the same language. The words and sentences we use have certain meanings in the language and we use them in those meanings. To so use them involves conforming to an established practice with these words and sentences. Within this practice, depending on what we intend to say, when we have uttered a word or sentence we commit ourselves for the future in the sense that going on in certain ways in what we say and do is part of meaning our words in their established sense – as was our intention. This is part of speaking, and what I am referring to are the speakers' actions and reactions – what they do, including how they go on in their use of words. People conform to these practices because they have been taught to do so since their childhood, and because the interdependence between the language of a community and the various practices, activities and institutions that make up its life, leave them no alternative in which they can find sense.[1]

But are there certain *beliefs* that people assent to as part of speaking a particular language, beliefs which they are not at liberty to question or check while they speak that language? Beliefs that lie at the basis of the speakers' speech and thought, constituting its bedrock? In *On Certainty* Wittgenstein argues not only that we learn to speak and act in harness, but also that learning to speak involves acquiring certain convictions. We have seen, for instance, that the concept of physical object is what Wittgenstein calls a 'logical concept' and that the existence of physical objects *is* the existence of what Wittgenstein calls a 'grammar' – a form of speaking within which certain words have sense, a way of acting and reacting in the weave of which these words are used, a context of action and interaction where the words in question are stationed. Thus to say that physical objects have a continued existence, for instance, is to utter a 'grammatical remark'. This is something which the child learns in learning to speak, though indirectly. So Wittgenstein writes:

> When a child learns language, it learns at the same time what is to be investigated and what not. When it learns that there is a cupboard in the room, it isn't taught to doubt whether what it sees later on is still a cupboard or only a kind of stage set. (§472)
>
> Just as in writing we learn a particular basic form of letters and then vary it later, so we learn first the stability of things as the norm, which is then subject to alterations. (§473)
>
> Children do not learn that books exist, that armchairs exist, etc., etc., – they learn to fetch books, to sit in armchairs, etc., etc.

Later, questions about the existence of things do of course arise. 'Is there such a thing as a unicorn?' and so on. But such a question is possible only because as a rule no corresponding question presents itself . . . (§476)

Unless the child had learnt to fetch books and sit in armchairs he could not question the existence of things in particular situations, he could not understand the question, 'Is there such a thing as a unicorn?', 'Did Pegasus ever exist?'. Unless he did, an existential affirmation would make no sense to him. It is in learning to fetch things, etc., etc., that he acquires the grammar within which certain questions and answers make sense. He not only learns to fetch the book he can see on the shelf, but also the book upstairs from which his father read him a story the day before. He doesn't learn that the book hasn't disappeared, or is still there, he 'swallows this consequence down together with *what* it learns.'[2]

'Books and the like don't just disappear': This is something one can hardly say. It is something on which so much of what we say and do rests and our arguments pivot. For instance, the librarian says: 'I note that the book named on this card was returned to the library yesterday and it has not been checked out since then. Therefore it must be here, go and look for it.' This is a proper conclusion under the circumstances because one is talking about books, reasoning within a particular grammar. The child learns to draw conclusions like this one. He learns not to ask a man who earlier reported seeing pink mice where the mice have got to. What the child learns in this way shows itself in the way he conducts himself in his speech and reasonings and actions. If what is in question can be described as a 'belief', then it is one that belongs to one's 'frame of reference'. But this doesn't make it part of a theory for 'interpreting the world'.

Contrast 'Books and the like do not disappear' with 'The vision has disappeared', or 'The water you were boiling has disappeared'. We can think and say the latter kind of thing against a background of things we can identify and reidentify and regard as relatively continuous and stable. Without the framework which makes this possible we could not speak of things disappearing, nor could we speak of anything continuing to exist.[3]

What Wittgenstein characterises as 'belonging to our frame of reference' is a very mixed bag. It is not always clear that what can be so characterised forms part of the basis of our speech and thought, for example 'As children we learn facts; e.g. that every human being has a brain, and we take them on trust. I believe that there is an island, Australia, of such-and-such a shape, and so on and so on. I believe that I had great-grand parents, etc.'[4] Wittgenstein comments: 'The child learns by believing the adult. Doubt comes *after* belief.'[5] He is not saying that what I thus learn is immune from doubt: 'I learned an enormous amount and accepted it on human authority, and then I found some things confirmed or disconfirmed by my own experience.'[6] But 'the continued existence of physical objects', 'the uniformity of nature' – are these truths I find confirmed by my experience, or the experience of others? No. When Wittgenstein speaks of such facts as that every human being has a brain, that water doesn't freeze when heated, he is suggesting that they constitute *for us* the place on which we stand when we raise questions and doubts, advance hypotheses and inquire about their truth: 'I have a world-picture. Is it true or false? above all it is the substratum of all my inquiring and asserting.'[7] 'Water doesn't freeze when heated.' To give that up we would have to modify our physics fundamentally. On this point Wittgenstein and Quine are in agreement. But would it have repercussions for the language we speak? There is no sharp line between a modification of the things we say *in* an unchanging language and a modification *of* the language itself in certain respects.

Wittgenstein says that 'learning is based on believing'.[8] But to believe in this sense you have to be pretty far ahead in language. And that, namely learning to speak, involves acquiring convictions which find expression in our actions and in our use of words, and these go unmentioned in our use of words. What is in question are not convictions about the reality we use our language to speak about or describe. They are convictions which determine what counts as reality and what as only appearance.

It is true, of course, that what concepts we develop makes a difference to the way we see things, to the aspects under which things present themselves to us. Certainly investigators in physics and in other disciplines of research and learning do develop new concepts and extend our language. On this point I would agree with Quine. But it is *within* a language that concepts are developed or modified. Such developments, and the change in our vision of things that goes with them, presuppose an ongoing language, an existing grammar, one which is neutral with regard to the rival visions which belong to competing theories. It is true that this grammar is not something independent of, something over and above, the concepts of the language. So modifications in the latter cannot be altogether dissociated from the grammar in question; they cannot leave that grammar intact. But still this does not mean, as Quine thinks, that grammar is indistinguishable from theory.

Roughly, one could make a three-part division, with no sharp, hard-and-fast lines in between: (i) We have descriptive, factual propositions of various kinds framed in a language. We utter them to say things which need not be true, and which if true could be false. *Some* of these propositions and truths (when they are true) presuppose a theory. (ii) We have theories which suggest various ways of looking at things and investigating them. Their acceptability in the end depends on their contribution to our understanding of the things we talk about and describe in our language and on the truth of the propositions they enable us to assert on particular occasions. (iii) There is the language and the grammar within which we distinguish between what is true and what is false, what is acceptable and what is not.

Does a theory, such as we find in physics, tell us anything? If we can regard it as a method or means of representation which enables us to describe various kinds of thing, then that far we can say that the theory itself does not tell us anything. Thus a system of co-ordinates does not tell one anything; it is the graph or curve which one plots on it that may do so – e.g. tell one how the crime rate in a particular society at a particular time varied with some other phenomenon, say the rise in unemployment. But we must not forget that even if it is true that it is a theory which makes it possible for physicists to frame experiments, nevertheless the acceptability of the theory depends ultimately on results of experiments. In this respect what analogy there is between a theory and a language breaks down, or becomes tenuous.

We do not adopt a language, nor do we construct the language we speak. To do so would be like trying to construct from scratch the ground on which we stand and walk. Quine appreciates this; he does not say that one can build oneself a ship at sea, but only that one can rebuild it piece-meal. Presumably one would wish to rebuild it because the ship was leaky – at least this is one possible reason. It is an intelligible one since ships are meant to float. But what is language meant to do? We cannot speak of the aims and purposes of language as we can speak of the purpose or function of ships. Language is not a means to anything – a means of communication, in the way that telephones are a means of communication. One could improve telephones with a view to improving communication; one could try to reduce crackle and fuzziness. Here the aim or purpose which the telephone serves is *external*, and that is why we can speak of the telephone, or the British telecom network of telephones, as serving it well or badly. But the aim with which one may try to improve a way of speaking, the standards with which one evaluates it when one describes it as satisfactory – these belong to language, they are *internal* to it.

What one may find unsatisfactory here is a way of speaking within the language one speaks – thus T. S. Eliot: 'that was a way of speaking, not very satisfactory'. What is in question is the inventive use of language to convey some vision or perception which conventional use has blunted in the speakers. This blunting is sometimes portrayed in caricature by talented dramatists like Harold Pinter. I am thinking of his portrayal of the way language has come to be used without saying anything, how in it people can no longer find anything to say. When that happens the poet may have to try and get away from phrases that have become *cliché*, and even whole ways of speaking, in an attempt to say something. But the possibility of doing so comes from the language, and the poet draws his vitality from poetic traditions which belong to it. It is the same with science and conceptual leaps within it.

Quine stresses the *practical* purposes which such developments serve. Wittgenstein too stresses the *work* which language does and the tendency in the philosopher and the formal logician to forget this: 'The sign-post is in order – if, under normal circumstances, it fulfils its purpose.'[9] To elaborate an example of Wittgenstein:[10] If someone asks you the way to the hospital, you may point to the right or to the left according to which way the hospital lies. But if you were to point both to the right and to the left he would not know which way to go. We would say that the directions you have given him were contradictory. But if the street was circular then these would be alternative directions and they would not contradict each other. Whether or not they are contradictory and should, therefore, be avoided depends on the circumstances. Wittgenstein says that the formal logician who is interested in building a system which stands above the changing circumstances in which we use language should be reminded that 'it is for practical, not for theoretical purposes, that the disorder is avoided'.[11] He makes this remark in the course of a discussion of contradictions in the foundations of mathematics. As I understand him, Wittgenstein thinks that there is something *artificial* about these foundations. He thinks that the philosophical logician's worry, for instance Russell's, about the contradictions which can be derived from these comes from misunderstanding: Whether or not contradictions can be derived from the so-called foundations of mathematics, if the mathematics itself serves us well in the various calculations we perform by means of it, then there can be nothing wrong with it. These purposes are practical: Counting – and that means counting in the way we do – has proved to pay.[12]

Whom has it proved to pay? Speakers of a language with a complex way of life such as ours. Wittgenstein stresses the two way dependence there is between the language and the life in question. The practical purposes and interests in terms of which the notion of payment is to be understood are *internal* to that language, life and culture, the language of which mathematics is a 'suburb', the life in the weave of which mathematics is used. This is where Wittgenstein differs, and differs radically from Quine. For Quine the purposes of science, as this has developed in Western society, are the purposes of language; or rather they are the purposes to which any adequate language has to conform. So much for Quine's relativism. The purposes are the practical purposes of science, and language has to conform to them if it is to be adequate. Thus language is a part of science – the scientific activity of man which stands at the pinnacle of his development. Hence Quine's declaration that the concepts of science are superior to the religious concepts of the early Greeks.[13]

The presupposition here is that the two sets of concepts and the languages to which they belong (Western scientific language and early Greek religious language) serve the same purpose which must, therefore, be external to both. Epigrammatically one could put the difference between Quine and Wittgenstein by saying that for Quine language is an instrument of science, whereas for Wittgenstein science is an enterprise, a mode of thinking, which is an offshoot, a development of one use of language among others. It has acquired a prominence in our culture which it has not always had in other cultures. That does not make our culture superior to such other cultures. We cannot say that 'understanding nature', or 'promoting survival', is the purpose which language serves. Rather men have many purposes which they could not have had without language and the kind of life that is inseparable from the use of language; and they use language in their attempt to promote these purposes. That of understanding nature is one of these; but language has not developed in order to serve this purpose, or any other.

When Quine speaks of the *utility* of a word or concept and asks whether we should admit the word or concept ('Will the consequences of admitting it be to our advantage?') he forgets that the standards of utility he puts into operation themselves come from our language and, therefore, cannot without circularity be made to measure the language. We never find this kind of circularity in Wittgenstein. In his writings the emphasis on *practical consequences* is directed against particular philosophical accounts – for instance, formalism in the philosophy of mathematics which tends to ignore the application of mathematics. Those remarks in Wittgenstein which may be misconstrued as expression of a pragmatist philosophy of language and of truth, if taken out of context, all occur in discussions of such questions as the justification of logical inference, the source of the necessity we find in logic and mathematics, whether contradictions in the foundations of mathematics vitiate mathematics, the status of mathematical propositions, whether grammar is responsible to reality. Where Wittgenstein speaks of utility and convenience he insists that the question of truth or justification does not arise and cannot do so. He insists that a technique or practice (counting, calculating our profits and losses in the way we do, arguing as we do, being guided by proofs in the way mathematicians are, etc.) is not itself true or false – any more than induction or scientific method is. The logic of such practices in each case is 'antecedent' to questions of truth and correspondence with a reality.[14] It is of the results we arrive at, the conclusions we draw that we speak as being true or false. The kind of comparison that helps us determine this, the standards to which our judgements of truth and falsity are responsible, are *internal* to the practices in question.

Thus Wittgenstein insists that 'mathematics as such is always measure, not the thing measured'.[15] 'If you know a mathematical proposition, that is not to say you yet know anything . . . If we agree, then we have only set our watches, but not yet measured any time.'[16] That the length of my ruler or foot is to be *called* a foot is not a statement that can be true or false. But once that is accepted, I can use my foot or ruler to measure the length and width of my room and order the appropriate number of tiles. Thus the statement that my room is 12' by 20' is a statement that may be true or false. Our use of the length of an average foot as a unit of measurement is convenient for these purposes, but not convenient for others – not for very long distances which we cannot easily cover on foot. So we have other units – miles, kilometres, etc. Similarly for propositions in arithmetic, say 2 + 2 = 4; 5 × 7 = 35. Wittgenstein compares them with e.g. '1ft = 12 inches'. His discussion is subtle and enlightening, but I am not now concerned with an appreciation of it.

Of counting, as we are familiar with it, Wittgenstein remarks: 'The *truth* is that counting has proved to pay.'[17] He is not claiming that to say that counting is true means that counting is useful. On the contrary, he is saying that it cannot be said of counting that it is true. What is true *about* counting, i.e. what could truly be said about it, is that it has proved to pay, *not* that there is a reality to which it conforms – as one may say of the proposition that there are 10 people in the room. Wittgenstein's alter-ego asks: 'Then do you want to say that "being true" means being usable (or useful)?' In other words: 'Are you putting forward a pragmatist account of truth?' Wittgenstein answers: 'No, not that, but that it can't be said of the series of natural numbers – any more than of our language – that it is true, but: that it is usable, and, above all, *it is used*.'[18]

Wittgenstein speaks about logical inference in the same way: 'Logical inference is a transition that is justified if it follows a particular paradigm, and whose rightness is not dependent on anything else.'[19] 'Rules of inference cannot be right or wrong.'[20] In Part I he asks: 'But what is the reality that "right" accords with here?'[21] Wittgenstein does not wish to deny that we may speak of rules of inference as 'right' as we do speak of propositions in pure mathematics as 'true'. As I put it in *Induction and Deduction*: 'They are at once rules of linguistic practice characterising different language-games [rules which enable me to make transitions from one proposition to another when, for instance, I calculate my expenses] and also instruments of language used in those language-games' (p. 168). To a lesser extent, perhaps, this is true of the rules of inference which logicians formulate. What I mean is that there is such a practice as pure mathematics and it has enormous consequences for the way we conduct our affairs and researches in many walks of life. The practice of the pure logician, on the other hand, is by and large confined to Departments of Philosophy and its consequences are very limited indeed – I mean its practical consequences. Therefore his formulae, in contrast with those of the mathematician, can hardly be described as 'instruments of language'. But if we can still describe e.g. a principle of inference as 'right' (and here Wittgenstein oscillates) then, he says, the reality with which 'right' accords is 'presumably a *convention*, or a *use*, and perhaps our practical requirements'.[22] But again his discussion of this question is both subtle and penetrating.[23]

For Quine, we have seen, there is no distinction between a theory and a language. His view is that a language is satisfactory and therefore acceptable if it is useful to us, if it serves our practical purposes adequately. He cheerfully describes himself as a *pragmatist* on this count. Wittgenstein, in contrast, speaks of practical matters, of what we find useful and convenient, as influencing developments in the language we already speak. But language, itself, is not something we can frame, construct, choose, adopt, reject, justify, consider as satisfactory or unsatisfactory. In *On Certainty*, thinking of language-games, he says: 'This game proves its worth. That may be the cause of its being played, it is not the ground' (§474). 'Language did not emerge from some kind of ratiocination' (§475). He remarks further down: A language-game 'is not based on grounds. It is not reasonable (or unreasonable). It is there – like our life' (§559). Once again questions of truth and justification are kept separate from pragmatic considerations.

4 Are there Universals?

I. ARE UNIVERSALS ENTITIES?

The question whether there are universals breaks up for Quine into several questions which he treats separately: Are there such entities as attributes, relations, classes, numbers, functions, meanings? (p. 9). He goes through a longer list in the last chapter of *Word and Object*.

As with 'Pegasus' there are two sorts of question he considers: (i) What does it mean to talk about numbers, classes, geometrical figures, etc.? This is what one may call an analytic question, that is a question regarding the analysis of certain concepts. (ii) Do we need to talk about classes, attributes, propositions, etc.? Can we say what we thus say differently? Can we dispense with any of these things? If we can, would this be a gain or a loss? Quine speaks of the second as an ontological question.

For Quine attributes, numbers, classes, etc., are instances of universals. If in our speech we quantify over them then we are committed to the view that there are abstract objects or entities alongside concrete ones – the latter including physical objects. As he puts it in his paper 'Reification of Universals': 'By treating predicate letters as variables of quantification we precipitate a torrent of universals' (p. 123). In *Word and Object* he refers to such philosophers as Ayer and Ryle who 'allow themselves not only abstract terms but even unmistakeable quantifications over abstract objects . . . and still blandly disavow, within the paragraph, any claim that there are such objects' (p. 241). He imagines them, when pressed, saying that abstract objects do not exist in the way that physical objects do. He thinks that this is a form of evasion and wishes to pin them down.

But, surely, all this talk about abstract objects and the existence of universals, or for that matter of e.g. attributes, needs

42

understanding. Who speaks about abstract objects and claims that there are universals alongside concrete individual things or entities? In what connection does he say these things? Someone may say: 'This is a dog, that is a dog, and so is that one over there. These things that we call dogs are particular and concrete things. I mean that we can point to them, see them, touch them, count them. Each occupies a particular place at a particular time and cannot be in two different places at the same time. Nor could two of them be in the same place at the same time. We group them together and call them by the same name because they belong to the same class. So there are classes as well as individual concrete things. Yet a class is an abstract object. You cannot see it or touch it, nor does it exist in space. Therefore there are abstract objects.'

I have no quick response to what is being said here. 'A dog is a particular.' This is meant to be a short-hand for 'A dog is something you can see, touch, point to, etc.' This is what Wittgenstein may have called a grammatical remark. It remarks on the kind of use words like 'dog' have. The word 'class' doesn't function like that. We do not use it of anything that we can point to. So far this says very little. But certainly it doesn't mean that we use it to name something, an entity, which has different properties. To say that 'a dog is something concrete', or that 'you can point to a dog' is not to ascribe a property to a dog. To say that a class is a special kind of entity, an abstract one, one that does not exist in space, is to invite confusion. It is better not to talk of a class as an entity at all. Otherwise one runs the risk of thinking that it is a queer sort of entity.

Quine says that someone who says, 'Some zo-ological species are cross-fertile' commits himself to recognising as entities the several species, abstract though they are' (p. 13). All right, he would have to admit that 'there are zo-ological species' meaning that 'animals can be classified into species'. But to say that animals can be, presumably usefully, so classified is not to say that alongside animals there are some other kind of entity, namely zoological species. Who on earth would think such a thing? Is it not plain that if 'There are zo-ological species' means 'Animals *can* be usefully classified into species', then what is asserted is not an existential claim?

'Are there species?' One answer would be: 'Well, zoologists talk about species.' If someone were to ask: 'And are they right to do so?', one answer would be: 'Well, it is not simply a whim on their part that they take certain animals in groups. They employ certain criteria and the results have been useful in what it has further enabled them to say.' Quine would be sympathetic to this answer.

But it is available in the case of zoological species because we are dealing with what one may call a theoretical concept. It is not available in the case of classes, attributes, relation or universals. What would it be to dispense with classes? In the last chapter of *Word and Object* (§55, 'Whither Classes?') Quine speaks of 'the power of the notion of class'. He is an admirer of Russell and he has in mind Russell's analysis of mathematics and the prominent role given there to the notion of class. Certainly one can raise questions about the merits of such an analysis or 'theory' as Quine calls it. Quine is all for retaining such an analysis and, therefore, the notion of class. All right. I am not now concerned with the merits of such an analysis. Certainly Wittgenstein, in the *Tractatus*, did not go along with it. He thought that 'the theory of classes is completely superfluous in mathematics' (6.031). But if one agreed with Wittgenstein, this would not mean that one was rejecting the notion of class. It would simply mean that one was critical of its use in a very special context.

'Is the notion of class useful? Can we dispense with it, and should we?' I do not understand what it would be to dispense with it. Classification is an important part of speaking; whenever one describes anything one classifies it in one form or another. Classification is inherent in the kind of generality which every description has. Without it there would be no description – which brings us to the heart of the philosophical problem of universals.

It concerns our use of words in general and general nouns in particular, and it asks what in reality corresponds to our use of words and our principles of classification. It seems that either some reality independent of our language does correspond to the meaning of our words and justifies their use in many particular cases, or otherwise the way we use them is arbitrary. That in reality which is supposed to correspond to the meaning of a word is a universal. It is itself *one* thing and justifies the use of the word in *many* cases. Because the one word is correctly used in many

cases, applied to many things, we can describe the word as a
general term. Since all words, including demonstratives and
proper names, have more than one application, their meaning
must have some form of generality in every case. So the problem
of universals asks what it is that gives words the generality
inherent in their meaning.

What does the question 'Are there universals?' ask? It is not an
existential question at all and is a confused way of asking many
different things. Take the proposition 'Tom is just'. Someone
may say: 'According to this proposition there is someone who is
just, and there is something that Tom is, namely just. Therefore,
anyone who asserts it is committed to recognising that there
are individual men, like Tom, and in addition that there are
universals like justice.' 'Is there such a thing as justice?' I can
easily imagine very different questions being asked by these
words. Thus imagine these words in the mouth of someone who
has suffered one injustice after another. He is asking whether men
are ever just. His experiences have disillusioned him, and he sees
around him only men who have been corrupted by power and
self-interest, or who are cowards. It doesn't seem to him that this
is inevitable, but it certainly strikes him as being the case. Plato
then comes along and, at first, it looks at if he is going to bring
some sanity and sense of proportion to our poor embittered man.
He says that men are a mixture of good and evil, of strengths and
weaknesses, and then in words that seem paradoxical he says that
'there can be no justice in the world, or in this life, that we must
be dead before we know justice'. I do not intend to discuss this
claim now. It has nothing to do with the problem of universals.
But I should say that Plato's claim is that justice is incompatible
with worldliness and attachment. He is not saying that men
cannot be just or know justice. He is saying that they cannot do so
until they transcend everything in themselves which attaches
them to worldliness. This is at once a moral claim and a
philosophical one – a profound remark about the *concept* of
justice.[1]

To return to poor old Tom who is said to be just. I imagined
someone saying: 'There is something which Tom is, namely just.
Therefore justice exists; and justice is a universal. Therefore
universals exist.' Compare with Moore's proof of an external
world.[2] Quine may retort that reference to justice is 'an avoidable

manner of speaking'. In other words, to say that men are sometimes just is not to say that there is something, namely justice, for them sometimes to be; it is to say that men sometimes *act justly*, or in a just manner. We have particular actions, and justice is one way in which some resemble each other. If A resembles B, we do not have three things, namely A, B, and the resemblance between A and B. This would be like : 'He came home with two things: 5 pence in his pocket and a nice smile on his face.' Russell may retort: Are there not resemblances then, and are not resemblances universals? Quine would, I imagine go along with that. He might say: I do not wish to deny that there are universals; I am concerned to determine which universals exist: What is the minimum number of universals without which we could not get along conveniently?

But why should Quine wish to dispense with attributes, as opposed to resemblances – attributes such as 'redness', 'doghood' and 'whiteness', and also 'justice'? He says: ' ''Some dogs are white'' says that some things that are dogs are white; and, in order that this statement be true, the things over which the bound variable 'something' ranges must include some white dogs, but need not include doghood or whiteness' (p. 13). So you can get along without whiteness and doghood and justice and redness. But what on earth does this mean except that you do not use the words 'redness' and 'justice', but simply speak of things as red and men as just?

But what is the harm in speaking of the redness of a tomato or of a man's love of justice? The answer is: We think that redness is in a tomato somewhat as its juice is in it.[3] In other words, we shall be liable to suppose that it is an ingredient, one that we can extract from the tomato as we may distil alcohol from alcoholic beverages.[4] Quine says something similar: 'The words ''houses'', ''roses'', and ''sunsets'' are true of sundry individual entities which are houses and roses and sunsets, and the word ''red'' or ''red object'' is true of each sundry individual entities which are red houses, red roses, red sunsets; but there is not, in addition, any entity whatever, individual or otherwise which is named by the word ''redness'', nor, for that matter, by the word ''househood'', ''rosehood'' or ''sunsethood'' ' (p. 10).

Quine means that redness is not something over and above red houses, red roses or red sunsets. But then Quine's ontological question 'Does redness exist?', or 'Does justice exist?', is asking whether redness is something over and above red things, or whether justice is anything over and above just men and just actions. And this is not an existential question, like 'Are there just people still on the face of the earth, and have they not all been corrupted in one way or another?' It is an analytic, conceptual question, like Berkeley's 'Is Matter anything but ideas?' which Wisdom compared with 'Is the average man anyone over and above individual men?'

We see that 'dispensing with attributes' is not reducing the number of universals to be admitted into our ontology. It is opposing one sort of view or philosophical account of the generality of words. To reject that account, to advance an alternative one, is not to put forward a different conceptual scheme – as Quine claims. 'Realism' and 'Nominalism', despite what Quine claims, are philosophical positions, and they are *neutral* with regard to the language we speak. To describe what Quine suggests, in opposition to his fictitious philosopher McX, as 'dispensing with attributes' is very misleading.

There is nothing wrong with attributes, and nothing wrong with a language which speaks of justice, honesty, rectitude, and the redness of a woman's cheeks. What is rejected by the Anti-realist is the idea that the redness of red things is like a coat of paint on them, that red things are red by virtue of the redness in them. When you drop a red solvent in a liquid it turns red. The idea opposed is that it is in this way that the redness in red things make them red. Wittgenstein referred to this as the idea of universals as ingredients. What this idea is and what is objectionable about it needs consideration.[5] And one also needs to be clear who it harms and where it does harm.[6]

My immediate point, however, is this. When philosophers discuss and debate the question whether there are physical objects they are concerned with a philosophical idea (model, picture, simile) regarding a pretty fundamental aspect or feature of language – an idea that is bound up with our difficulties in knowing what to make of it, although we understand the language perfectly well. This philosophical idea is not an idea (concept, posit) intended to explain the grouping of our sensations, and to represent the way these change in a way we find easy to grasp. Likewise, when philosophers discuss and debate the question whether there are universals or attributes, they are concerned with a philosophical idea (model, picture, simile) regarding the generality of the words in any language. Just as it doesn't make sense to question, deny or assert the existence of physical objects, so likewise it doesn't make sense to question, deny or assert the existence of attributes. At least to do so cannot be what it appears to be.

II.   REALISM AND NOMINALISM

Realism is the philosophical view that there is something in things, or outside them, something that exists independently of language, which our use of words reflects. What gives our words their generality is our use of them on countless different occasions, in a great many instances. The realist view is that there must be something which unifies these occasions, binds together these instances, and that it is what does so which constitutes the basis of our language. In the case of common nouns such as 'table' and 'dog', and adjectives such as 'red' and 'just', it constitutes the basis of our classifications. The two forms which realism has taken traditionally are to be found in Plato and Aristotle, though I take Plato's 'theory of forms' to speak to questions many of which have little to do with 'the problem of universals'. According to the Platonic version universals are essences which exist *outside* things: what relates different things to each other as things of the same kind are the relation of each ('approximation') to a common essence or paradigm. According to the Aristotelian version universals are *in* the different things we call by the same name. Thus 'redness' or 'justice' is supposed to be the name of something (a common essence) which different red things or different just acts resemble in different degrees (Platonic version), or the name of something (a common property) which they all possess (Aristotelian version). This common essence or property is what determines our classification and governs our use of the word in question. According to Plato it exists in separation from the things classified; and according to Aristotle it can at least be thought in separation from them.

The Nominalist rejects this idea. But there are, in fact, different forms of nominalism, some more extreme, some less. According to the most extreme form, which is perhaps the only position that deserves to be called nominalism, a name is all that different things that we call by the same name have in common.

In other words, the application of every name, and indeed of every word, is arbitrary. It is not based on any reality outside purely human conventions.

According to a more moderate version of it, things that we call by the same name do not share any common properties, but they resemble each other. All things resemble each other in many different ways. We choose some of these resemblances in grouping some things together. This view is to be found in Locke: Universals are 'creatures of the understanding', the principles in accordance with which we classify things are man-made, but they are based on a reality that is independent of language. This is how Professor Mackie puts it in his book *Problems from Locke*:

> Though he (Locke) says . . . that 'the *sorting* of things under names is the *workmanship of the understanding*', he states quite clearly that the mind has something real and natural to work from, namely the multitude of objective resemblances between things (p. 112).

And again:

> We can largely agree with Locke that . . . though nature supplies the similitudes, it supplies far more of them than we use: it is by the work of the mind that some resemblances and not others are recorded in language (p. 136).

This position has some affinity to realism. It is in fact a form of realism, since it speaks of something independent of language, namely resemblances, accounting for our use of words, if only partly, and explaining their generality. Locke's view thus is that universals are man-made, but made within limits dictated by an independent reality.

It would be of interest to note that there is a two-way connection between the Platonic view and the Lockean view. First Plato, unlike Aristotle, claims that we can find no more than various degrees of resemblance between the 'objects of sense' that we talk about. He does not wish to speak of them as sharing a common property: 'No two logs are perfectly equal' (*Phaedo*). In this respect one may liken Plato to Locke. But, secondly, Plato wishes to contrast 'objects of sense' with 'purely intelligible objects', such as we find in mathematics. It is there that we find perfect equality. Locke makes the same distinction when he talks of classifications that are based on the 'nominal essences' of the things classified and classifications based on their 'real essences'.

I would like to discuss this briefly because it has a bearing on what I am going to say. The *essence* of a kind K is supposed to be a set of properties E such that –

(i) anything that lacks E cannot be of kind K (whatever other properties it may have) and

(ii) anything which has E cannot be of any kind other than K (whatever other properties it may lack). Thus

(a) Where a, b, c constitute the *real essence* of K, then all other properties which K has belong to it *by virtue of this essence* – i.e. belong to it essentially or necessarily. For instance if d is a property of K, then anything that has E, in other words a, b, c, *must* have d – i.e. anything that has E *cannot* fail to have d. That is d is an *inseparable property* of anything that has a, b, and c, i.e. of anything that makes it a K, say a circle or a triangle.

(b) Where a, b, c constitute the *nominal essence* of K, this is not so. The connection between a thing's possession of a, b, c, by virtue of which we *call* it K, e.g. 'iron', and its possession of d, e.g. obedience to the loadstone, is *contingent* or *accidental*.

So – The *real essence* of K is that without which X *could not be* of kind K.
It is that with which X *could not but be* of kind K – i.e. *must* be of kind K.
It is that without which X *ought not to be classified* as a K.
It is that without which we would be *wrong* to classify X as of kind K.

According to Locke those things we call 'gold' are classified by us as gold in accordance with a *nominal essence*. We say: 'Anything that has properties a, b, c, d is going to be called "gold".' We pick on these properties because as a matter of fact we find them together. But we need not have classified together all things that have just these properties. Since all things that have these properties vary in many of their other properties we could have classified them differently.

Thus supposing we had nine objects with the following properties:

(1) abcdefg   (2) abcdlmg   (3) abcdnmf
(4) abcdhij   (5) abcdklm   (6) abcdcfl
(7) abedfg   (8) abeflm   (9) abefkl

If we make abcd into a defining property of K, i.e. the nominal essence of K, then we could group 1, 2, 3, 4, 5, 6 together and call them K. If, on the other hand, we made abef into a defining property of K', then we could group 1, 6, 7, 8, 9 together and call them K'.

If, on the other hand, we knew the *real essence* of K, then no such choice would be open to us. According to Locke the nominal essence of triangle coincides with its real essence. He says that, therefore, there is nothing 'loose' about the way the properties essential to triangularity are united into the real essence of that kind. This union is not determined by human choice. Since they are united essentially they cannot be found in any variation. As Locke puts it: 'If things were distinguished into species according to their real essences, it would be as impossible to find different properties in any two individual substances of the same species, as it is to find different properties in any two circles or two equilateral triangles.'[7] But, Locke points out, 'we sort and name substances by their nominal and not by their real essences'.[8]

Thus the contrast, in Locke, between substances, thus sorted and named, and geometrical figures is very closely connected with Plato's contrast between 'objects of sense' and 'purely intelligible objects'.

Take the geometrical circle. The mathematician's reflections on it issue into *theorems* which once recognised are seen to admit no alternative. The truth of these theorems is independent of what measurements reveal in particular cases. It is thus fixed independently of the results of such measurements. The carriage wheel in front of me, for example, is subject to change. My description of it must be checked against its actual features to see that it is true. When it changes with wear and tear my description will have to be modified if it is to remain true. But the theorems which 'describe' the geometrical circle are timelessly true. Their truth is independent of the vagaries of nature.

Further, once these theorems are known, we can deduce from

them, without further ado, *everything* that is true of the circle. That is the mathematician's 'description' of the circle encompasses *everything* there is to know about it. It is thus a description of what the word 'circle', as the mathematician means it, signifies – in other words, a definition. I put 'description' in inverted commas since it is not a description in the ordinary sense, a description of what we use the word to talk about – the shape of wheels, the cross-section of barrels, etc. It is rather a 'description' of the word's meaning, which some philosophers have referred to as an idea or abstract entity. Because it encompasses *everything* there is to know about a circle, it seemed to Socrates that the search for this kind of 'description', or definition, one that captures the essence (Locke: the real essence) of the kind of thing which the word defined names, is a search for ideal knowledge. For once one grasps this essence, one knows *all there is to know* about the circle.

If, on the other hand, one goes about measuring circular objects, one will keep finding new truths. The knowledge which these add up to will forever be *incomplete* or partial, since one can always add to it. It can be acquired only in a piece-meal way. The truths which comprise it hang together only 'loosely', as Locke would put it. They do not constitute an indissoluble whole. One cannot understand, Locke would say, why the objects one studies thus have the features which one discovers in them. What one's examination reveals can give one no cast iron guarantee about what is to be found in new instances, in cases not yet examined.

So Locke would say that where we are ignorant of the real essence of the kind of thing we are studying we cannot be sure that we are not faced with an arbitrary collection of properties, i.e. properties which *we* have made into a basis of classification. Where we pick out just these properties to form a class (e.g. yellowness, malleability, solubility in aqua regia – in the case of gold) it may not correspond to a real essence. All things which have these properties will obviously have many others as well. But since these properties do not form an indissoluble whole, and so can exist apart from each other, we could have classified the things which have one or more of them differently.

This is not true of geometrical figures or kinds. For that without which a figure cannot be a circle is incompatible with or excludes that without which it cannot be a square. A figure cannot be at once both bounded by straight lines and also be circular. Whereas, in contrast, that without which an animal would not be called a 'cow' by us (e.g. horns and hoofs) is not incompatible with that without which it would not be called a 'dog' (e.g. being carnivorous). There could have been an animal which had horns and hoofs and ate meat, even though as a matter of fact such animals do not exist. Hence it may be that if we classified animals according to their diet they would fall into different groups from the ones into which they would fall if classified according to their physical make-up. In other words, alternative modes of classification are possible here. Whereas, in contrast, whatever geometrical features one makes into one's basis for classifying plane figures one will inevitably end up with the same classification of them. So, in Euclidean geometry, we have no option about the way we classify plane figures, and the kinds into which they are classified are not subject to change – since they cannot be without the properties which make them into the kind of figure each is. As Locke puts it:

> All things that exist, besides their Author, are liable to change; especially those things we are acquainted with and have ranked into bands under distinct names or ensigns . . . But essences being taken for ideas established in the mind, with names annexed to them, they are supposed to remain steadily the same, whatever mutations the particular substances are liable to.[9]

The latter, he says, 'are all ingenerable and incorruptible. Which cannot be true of the real constitution of things, which begin and perish with them'.[10]

I have said something about the notion of *essence* in connection with classification and the naming of kinds because the philosophical claim that 'There are universals' is often tantamount to the claim that the *meaning* of a general name is, or corresponds to, the *essence* of the kind of thing it names, the essence which makes each thing the kind of thing it is. It is this essence that determines the classification in question and the correct application of the name, giving it the kind of generality it has. The claim, 'There are universals', is thus the claim that this account is correct. This is the Realist position.

The words 'There are universals' are also uttered by philosophers who wish to assert that 'There are properties' or that 'Words have generality' – as if this is something that can be asserted. They feel called upon to do so because they think that it can be and has been denied. The words thus purport to assert a platitude, but come from confusion. Whereas, in the former case, they do not purport to assert a platitude at all, but something questionable. This has been questioned by Nominalists, and also by philosophers who are not nominalists. Thus Berkeley rejected Locke's *abstract ideas*, just as he rejected his notion of a substratum, the support of the sensible qualities of physical objects. Abstract ideas are the mental counterpart of the essences, real and nominal, which are supposed to enable us to classify things, to identify them as of this or that kind, and to name them. Since Locke treated all words as names and thought of their meanings as ideas, abstract ideas for him are meanings of general words – including common nouns.

Berkeley rejects the view that we need abstract ideas as intermediaries to use one word to name many things, to apply it on a multitude of occasions. Similarly, though obviously there are many differences, Wittgenstein rejects the view that we need a common property or essence to use a general term. But that does not make him a nominalist. He certainly thinks that the idea that what is at issue here is ontological in character comes from confusion. H. H. Price thinks that what is at issue between the realist and the nominalist is partly ontological, in the sense that it is concerned with claims about some very general features of the world, viz. whether or not 'there are recurrent characteristics in the world'.[11] So does Quine, although his conception of ontology is very different from Price's.

To see how Quine is wrong it is important to be clear about *what* is being rejected by the anti-realist and *why* it is being rejected, and whether this leaves us in deficit – i.e. without something which we have had, something we now have to get on without. Let us consider this briefly in the case of Wittgenstein.

III.   WITTGENSTEIN'S ANTI-REALISM

Wittgenstein considers the example of a person expecting someone to tea: What does his expectation consist of? What is it that makes us say, justify us in saying that he is *expecting* someone to tea? Is it the same in every case? Until we actually look at *particular cases*, the question put in general terms inclines us to say:

'Since we are talking about the same thing, namely expecting, what makes us use the same word in the different cases where we do so must be the same thing.' This is impeccable insofar as it is a tautology: 'What makes us use the same word, e.g. 'expecting', in different cases must be the same thing, namely expectation – that each case is a case of a person expecting someone.' But the question was: What makes each case a case of that? On bringing vividly before our minds such individual cases we see that there is a great deal of variety, many differences, and no single feature or set of features that remain the same from one case to the other.

(i) Wittgenstein's first point is that, as a matter of fact, it is different features, different details that make us speak of the same thing in different cases. This shows that what justifies us in using a word in a particular case is not necessary to the case being of the kind in question. This contradicts the essentialist thesis which ties together meaning and necessity. So although the different cases in question manifestly share no common feature or features we nevertheless find it natural to use the same word in them. This cannot be, therefore, what it takes to use a general word.

(ii) To the person who says, 'There *must* be a common feature or features', Wittgenstein retorts: 'Don't think, but look.'[12] He means that there is no 'must' about it. He considers someone who is not satisfied by what he sees: 'True, what we see are variations, differences. But there must be an underlying identity of feature or features all the same.' Wittgenstein retorts: If our correct use of the word is based on what we do not see when we look, how come that despite our not seeing it we manage to use the word correctly in case after case? This hidden essence on which our use of a general word is supposed to be based is, therefore, a myth.

(iii) Wittgenstein's third point is that even if we were to find some common property in the different cases where we use the same word, why should *that* be what makes each a case of for example expectation?[13] He argues that the features we notice in particular cases add up to what is in question *only in certain surroundings*. If one changes these surroundings the case, very often, will no longer be a case of what is in question. That is the features could not have been *sufficient* to make it a case where we are justified in using the general word. But neither are they *necessary*. For one may find that if one takes away those features but keeps the surroundings, one still has a case of the kind in question, e.g. one of expectation. Wittgenstein illustrates this beautifully in his consideration of facial expression in *The Brown Book*, Part II, pp. 145–6. In what he says here the crudity of the philosophical idea sticks out like a sore thumb.

What Wittgenstein aims to illustrate is that what makes a case one of a particular kind, what gives it the general features we see in it, the aspect under which we see it, is not something beneath the surface, but the 'surface' itself – the surface details and the surrounding circumstances. The idea that it is something else, something that remains the same from one case to another, something constant beneath the details that vary from case to case, is the idea of 'universals as ingredients' as Wittgenstein calls it – the idea that redness is in the tomato as the juice in it (H. H. Price), that 'beauty is an ingredient of all beautiful things as alcohol is of beer and wine, and that we therefore could have pure beauty, unadulterated by anything that is beautiful'.[14]

The model for such neat ingredients is to be found in mathematical concepts and what it is they are supposed to mean – *vide* Plato's forms and Locke's real essences. Thus in the *Phaedo* Socrates rightly contrasts mathematical equality and physical equality: 'Then those equals and the equal itself are not the same.' But then it seems to him that in the mathematical case we have equality pure and neat ('the equal itself'), while in the physical case we have equality adulterated: 'No two logs are perfectly equal.' There are, of course, real differences between mathematical and physical equality. But Socrates misrepresents these when he thinks of physical equality as somehow less perfect, more crude, as a kind of poor imitation of mathematical equality.

What exercises him is that the employment of the term 'equals' is not governed in the physical cases by strict criteria, as in pure mathematics. And it seems that where there are no such criteria, i.e. where a word cannot be defined in terms of the necessary and sufficient conditions of its employment, its meaning has been only imperfectly determined, or not determined at all. Wittgenstein asks how we should explain to someone what a game is. He says that we should describe some games to him and add: 'This and *similar things* are called "games".' He adds: 'And do we know any more about it ourselves?'[15] Yet it seems that unless we do, we do not really know what a game is, or what we mean by 'game'.[16] If we know it, if the word means anything, it seems that we must be able to extract the *essence* of gamehood, to formulate the necessary and sufficient conditions of the word's application. The idea is that when we are given the meaning of a word (such as 'game' or 'red') we are given a blue-print which guarantees its application in case after case, and that nothing that falls short of this can give us the word's meaning. The definitions of mathematical, geometrical terms satisfy this condition.

'This *and similar things* are called "games".' We feel that we have not been given sufficient guidance: You have told me that this is called a game, that it is correct to call it a game. But you have not told me in what other cases I can correctly apply this word. You have not prevented me from going wrong, from not knowing whether this thing I come across, e.g. solitaire, is a game or not. You have left me on my own and without support. If you had given me the *meaning* of the word I would not have been in this predicament.[17] I have been given examples, but I have not been told the mark by which I can identify them. If I am able to do so in new cases this is what I need to know: the thing I mean by the word 'game', the essence of gamehood, the respects in which all games are alike. This is what a definition ought to capture.

This seems (wrongly) essential to our understanding of any term,[18] and it seems that it is, moreover, available in the case of mathematical terms. The supposed essence of things which makes them the kind of thing they are and enables us to name them is thus a shadow cast on our language by mathematics. In rejecting it as a *myth* Wittgenstein is combating the tendency to think of language as an exact calculus. This is very far from rejecting an ontological claim.

In the *Theaetetus* Socrates seeks for a definition of 'knowledge' on the model of Theaetetus' answer about roots. What do the sides of the figures overleaf have in common? If they are all of the same kind, can we not define the kind in question? Of any number n, we can ask whether or not its root (square root) is commensurable with 1. We arrive at the answer in each case by *calculation*. The calculation establishes, proves that n is or is not rational, i.e. commensurable with 1. So Socrates speaks of 'a single character to embrace all that multitude' – that multitude of numbers that are not commensurable with 1, all irrational numbers.

He asks Theaetetus to take this as his *model* and 'to find a single formula that applies to the many kinds of knowledge'.[19] Such a formula will capture the 'essential nature' of the different things we call 'knowledge', 'the thing itself – knowledge – is' – as in the

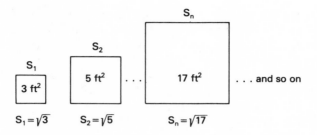

other case it will isolate the mark by which we can recognise, identify irrational numbers. He says: 'You do not suppose a man can understand the name of a thing, when he does not know what the thing is' (147B).

This is the misunderstanding which Wittgenstein is concerned to straighten: 'Do you want to say that I don't know what I am talking about until I can give a definition of a plant?'[20] The tendency to think that a blurred concept is no concept at all is part of the same misunderstanding.[21] Wittgenstein is not saying that concepts that are blurred cannot be made more definite. The concept of game does not have a sharp boundary, but 'we can draw such a boundary – for a special purpose: Does it take that to make a concept usable?'[22] Notice that if we can sharpen the boundary of a concept in a particular direction we do so for a special practical purpose. What this involves is removing *some* of the vagueness in the *application* of the term or concept. For instance, we may say: 'It is not domestic oil until it meets certain stringent requirements, passes certain tests; and anyone who calls it so and sells it under the name will be prosecuted.' The tests are perhaps specified in a leaflet, or some general description (instruction) is given of how they are to be carried out. Perhaps certain instruments, gauges, chemicals are specified. But how accurate are these instruments supposed to be? Will such-and-such a gauge be acceptable? There are thousands of questions that could be raised which the instructions never anticipated and so do not answer. If any one of them were to assume importance for practical purposes, the need would arise to formulate an answer to them. Doing so would be drawing a boundary, or making the existing boundary tighter. But for every such question answered a great many new ones could be asked – asked intelligibly, but not necessarily taken seriously. As Wittgenstein puts it: 'That is not to say that we are in doubt because it is possible for us to *imagine* a doubt.'[23] 'An explanation serves to remove or to avert a misunderstanding – one, that is, that would occur but for the explanation; not every one that I can imagine.'[24]

It is the same with giving a concept sharp boundaries in a certain range of its applications – the same as averting a contradiction, removing a misunderstanding, or meeting a doubt. It is not the concept itself that requires sharp boundaries in order to have meaning; *we* require it for special practical purposes. Wittgenstein argues that we cannot 'stop up all the cracks' and so remove all possible doubts as to whether a term is applicable in a particular case.[25] He imagines the case where I say 'There is a chair', go up to fetch it and it disappears from sight. But in a few moments we are able to see and touch it, and so on, though a little later it disappears again: What are we to say? Have we rules ready for such cases? And if not, do we miss them when we use the word 'chair'?[26] In *Zettel* he asks: 'How should we have to imagine a complete list of rules for the employment of a word? What do we mean by a complete list of rules for the employment of a piece of chess? Couldn't we always construct doubtful cases, in which the normal list of rules does not decide?' He goes on: 'The regulation of traffic in the streets permits and forbids certain actions on the part of drivers and pedestrians, but it does not attempt to guide the totality of their movements by prescription. And it would be senseless to talk of an "ideal" ordering of traffic which should do that . . . If someone wants to make traffic regulations stricter on some point or other, that does not mean that he wants to approximate to such an ideal' (§440).

We think that such an ideal is realised in logic and mathematics, and that insofar as our language deviates from it, it must be defective. But how is such an ideal realised in mathematics? Take an example from geometry: 'If it is a triangle, it must be a three-sided plane figure with straight edges; and if it is such a figure then it is necessarily a triangle. And so it would be correct to describe it as such.' Similar definitions are possible and can be given of the terms used in the definition: 'a straight line is the shortest path between two points' and '$3 = 2 + 1$', and similarly for the terms used in these definitions. Thus one word is defined in terms of others and those in terms of others still. But so far nothing has been said about how any of them is to be applied in a particular case. How, for instance, are we to establish that a given line is the shortest path between two points in a particular case? All right, it is a triangle *if* its sides are straight, and its sides are straight *if* they constitute the shortest path between the corners. These 'ifs' must be removed if we are to know when to say that a figure before us is a triangle. Yet they cannot be removed by further definitions. What I have in mind is sometimes referred to as 'giving an application to a calculus' or 'interpreting a calculus'. Wittgenstein argues that it is this application that gives meaning to the terms of the calculus – in this case, to the terms 'triangle', 'straight line', '3', etc. He says: 'It is essential to mathematics that its signs are also employed in civil life.'[27]

Put it like this: In mathematics, in geometry we have definitions, theorems which state e.g. the conditions necessary to a figure's being a triangle. These conditions, we might say, exemplify the *essence* of triangularity. Where they are satisfied it follows *deductively* that we can correctly talk of a triangle. Where this is so, we are necessarily justified in using the term 'triangle'. This is what attracts us because it makes us think that here at least we cannot go wrong, that we have been given the whole use of the word in one swoop – as we have not in the case of the word 'game' where we are merely told that 'this and similar things are called "games"'. What we overlook, however, is that we still have to decide or judge whether or not the conditions in question are satisfied anew in each particular case. Thus what we thought had been eliminated reappears.

So we are in the same position where we can extract an essence, e.g. in geometry, as the one we are in where we cannot do so. In other words, the essence we extract does not give us the support we had hoped for. We thought that once we have got hold of the essence, formulated a rule or a definition, we will be able for example to continue the series, go on to apply the word correctly in instance after instance without further ado. But, Wittgenstein argues, rules, formulae and definitions, examples and illustrations, can always be meant and so taken or understood in a variety of ways. Hence the statement of a rule or definition, the essence we have grasped in geometry, cannot *itself* give us a criterion of the right way to continue a series, the correct way to use a word.[28] As he puts it in *Zettel*: 'There is no such thing here as, so to say, a wheel that he is to catch hold of, the right machine which, once chosen, will carry him on automatically' (§304).

One could say: 'There is no essence or common structure that can guide us infallibly in our application of general terms.' 'There are no ethereal rails or tracks that can compel us in our deductive reasonings.' These two misunderstandings of what gives a term a general application and what makes a deductive conclusion follow from the premises with necessity are closely connected. The Nominalist wishes to combat the first misunderstanding and the Conventionalist wishes to combat the second. Only each goes wrong in his attempt to do so.

Let me put this point differently: In geometry we support the use of a term, e.g. 'triangle', deductively, and this pleases us. We then notice that this justification presupposes that the conditions from which the correct application of the term follows deductively are satisfied in the particular case. But the claim that they are satisfied cannot itself be supported deductively. Thus we can say that if this figure satisfied condition E then *necessarily* it is of kind K – a triangle. But does it satisfy it? Geometry itself is silent on this question and cannot decide it for us. In his paper 'Universals and Family Resemblances' Renford Bambrough puts this by saying that *no* concept can *ultimately* be explained in terms of necessary and sufficient conditions, that in *no* case can the application of a term be *ultimately* justified deductively.

It is in this sense that the idea that universals are properties essential to the application of general names is a myth. It should be clear that what is in question is not an unsatisfactory theory, such as we have in the sciences, but a misunderstanding of the logic of our language in the sense I have tried to explain. The words 'Universals do not exist' represent an attempt to reject this myth, to combat the misunderstanding embodied in it.

One who rejects it, however, is not committed to Nominalism: Although the many things we call games do not share any set of common properties, yet it is not for nothing that we call them 'games'. We are justified in calling them by the same name by the 'complicated network of similarities' that relate them to each other in the way Wittgenstein describes.[29]

The point which Wittgenstein is making with his simile of 'family resemblances', as I understand it, is this. There is no way of grasping or presenting the application of a word at one go and without reference to particular cases of its use or application. *In the end* instances, particular cases, are what we have to turn to and compare with each other. *In the end* the meaning of *any* word can only be gathered from the particular cases in which it is applicable

- whether or not the word is definable in terms of necessary and sufficient conditions as in mathematics.

I am thinking particularly of his discussion of the way we learn to continue mathematical series, to match objects to samples, to pick out particular kinds of object from among miscellaneous groups. 'One gives examples and intends them to be taken in a particular way. I do not, however, mean by this that he is supposed to see in those examples the common thing which I – for some reason – was unable to express; but that he is now to *employ* those examples in a particular way. Here giving examples is not an *indirect* means of explaining – in default of a better one.'[30] In other words there is nothing more fundamental than the giving of examples, something beneath or behind them which, if only we could get to it, would enable us to dispense with examples, to by-pass them.[31] I am suggesting that when Wittgenstein says that if we look at the different things we call by the same name we shall not see 'something common', but instead 'a complicated network of similarities', he is saying that if we wish to understand what gives a term its generality, what makes it applicable in many instances, we should look at the *instances* themselves, and not look for anything that stands apart from them. There is nothing here which we can examine in separation from the examples. Anything which at first sight seems to stand apart in this way, e.g. a rule, a definition, a sample of pure green, has itself to be understood, and the attempt to do so inevitably brings us down to the examples.

He is also saying that seeking the general features of a particular case, 'seeing the universal in the particular' *is* seeing the particular in relation to other things with which it can be compared. Seeing something under a certain aspect or as an instance of a certain kind *is* seeing it as related to other things, seeing it as being like other things in different ways.

But is this not a 'resemblance thesis of universals' – albeit a subtle version of it? I do not think so. Wittgenstein would have said that what we call 'similarity' and 'difference' varies from one language-game to another and so from one system of classification to another. Therefore similarities and differences cannot be made to constitute the *ultimate basis* of *any* classification, the *common basis* of different classification.

To claim that what similarities we perceive is relative to our language, however, is *not* to say that similarities are *man-made*.

They are no more man-made than the language we speak or the culture in which we judge, act and reason. In *The Brown Book* Wittgenstein imagines a people who differ from us in certain ways in their culture and education, and so in their habits of reacting to colours. They assimilate colours between which we distinguish, and distinguish between colours and shades we classify together (pp. 134–5). We can take part of such an example and develop it in certain ways. These people do not see transitions from one colour or shade to another and so never speak of shades of the same colour for instance. Perhaps they even lack this concept altogether. They take no interest in nature, never paint or contemplate natural scenes. Their talk of colour lacks some of the connections such talk has in our lives. Etc. Will it not be the case that a whole range of affinities and differences between colours, as we see them, will simply not exist for them? They simply will not see these. If *we* say that they are blind to these, we can mean no more than that *they* do not see what *we* see. There is nothing more ultimate, neutral between our different languages to enable us to mean more than this.

Wittgenstein also imagines someone who differs in his reactions to notes played on our musical scale. He is played the diatonic scale and asked whether he would say that he hears the same notes again at certain intervals. He says that he hears the same note alternately after every four or three notes. We say we hear the same note after every seven notes.[32] We might say that he is deaf to certain aspects of the notes *we* hear. But the reality of this aspect – the sameness of notes that are octaves of each other – depends on our reactions being shared and on much else in our life that surrounds that activity of making music and listening to it. If we say that he is deaf to certain aspects of music and thus imply the existence of something, a similarity, to which he is deaf, that is only because of the overwhelming agreement in reactions from which he is separated.

But now imagine him to be a member of a community of people who share his reactions, speak a language and take part in activities based on these reactions, and you can no longer think of them as having an 'incomplete' or 'limited' awareness of reality. Wittgenstein says that if we imagine a society of the feeble-minded we would do better to think of its people not as 'essentially incomplete' but under the aspect of 'a more primitive order'.[33] His point is that if there were a people who in their reactions resembled those among us we call feeble-minded, and if these people evolved a life and a language of their own, then in some respects their world would be different from the world in which we live. Some of the features of our world would not just be unmarked in their language; they would not be features to be marked at all.

Supposing we were asked: 'What do a note and its octave have in common?' Wittgenstein would say: 'It is no answer to say: "They have a certain affinity." '[34] He says: 'There is something remarkable about saying that we use the word "strain" for both mental and physical strain because there is a similarity between them. Should we say we use the word "blue" both for light blue and dark blue because there is a similarity between them? If you were asked "Why do you call this 'blue' also?", you would say "Because it *is* blue too." '[35]

Thus we use the word 'blue' to describe the colour of the sky, one of the colours of the French flag, and that of litmus paper when dipped in an alkaline solution. To say that we do so because we see certain similarities between these explains nothing. That is just a restatement of what we think needs explaining. Our calling them by the same name, 'blue', and our finding them similar, are on the same level. Neither is more fundamental than the other; they are just two sides of the same coin.

'But are we not right to call them "blue" – to call them by the same name? Are we not saying something true when we say that they are similar?' The answer is: It depends on what is being asked. In one kind of case we could say: Of course he is right; take the materials into the daylight and you will see that he is right. As if to say: Indeed they are the same colour. In another case, where these questions are an expression of philosophical unease, we could say: Of course, *we* see a similarity between these things: 'that is how our concepts take it.'[36] Of course we are right, for That is how we use the word 'blue'. But are we right to use it that way? I am suggesting that this last question comes from confusion, as does the answer: 'We are right if there is really a similarity between these things.' We wish to base our use of the word, i.e. the way we use it, on something more fundamental, something which we think will justify it. We have our mind focused on the justification of the use of the word in a particular case – such as when we say 'This is blue', or 'Though this seems green in this light, it is really blue'. Here the use of the word is taken for granted: 'Given the way we use the word "blue", i.e. given its correct use, this is blue.' What we are trying to do in the philosophical case is to try to justify that use itself, i.e. what in the ordinary example our justification takes for granted. That is to go round in a circle.

Wittgenstein brings this out well in one of his examples in *Zettel* while discussing the relation between grammar and reality: What is our basis or justification for grouping colours around four primary ones in the way we do? Does this reflect something about 'the world as it actually is'? 'Doesn't one put the primary colours together because there is a similarity among them?' Wittgenstein responds: 'If I say "there is a particular similarity among the primary colours" – whence do I derive the idea of this similarity? Just as the idea "primary colour" is nothing else but "blue or red or green or yellow" – is not the idea of that similarity too given simply by the four colours? Indeed, aren't they the same?' We resist the suggestion because it seems to make our grouping of colours, and therefore our concept of primary colour, into something *arbitrary*: 'Then might one also take red, green and circular together?' Wittgenstein's response is: 'Why not?'[37]

It is clear that Wittgenstein rejects the view that all classification rests ultimately on the similarities and differences with which Nature presents us independently of our systems of classification. We may have thought otherwise because we had been misled by his remark that although the things we call by the same name need have no one thing in common, 'they are related to one another . . . by a complicated network of similarities overlapping and criss-crossing'.[38] But now it may seem that he has adopted a nominalist position: 'We might have taken together red, green and circular.' That too is a misunderstanding. No doubt such a grouping strikes us as arbitrary. Just like that it would be arbitrary. But imagine a particular cultural background against which it makes sense, and it will no longer strike you as arbitrary.

In the *Investigations* Wittgenstein says that asking 'Is this object composite?' *outside* a particular language-game makes no sense (§47). This is just as true of the question 'What do these things have in common?' or 'Can they be intelligibly grouped together?'. Thus in response to the question 'What do these colours I am pointing to have in common?' Wittgenstein replies: The answer to this really ought to be 'I don't know what game you are playing.'[39] He then imagines a game: 'A shows B different patches of colours and asks him what they have in common. B is to answer by pointing to a particular primary colour.' Wittgenstein gives various examples where the answer is obvious. Then he gives an example where in this game the answer is 'They have nothing in common' – for the colours pointed to are primary colours: pure red and pure green. From within the game described to group these colours together it looks arbitrary – very much as the grouping together of red, green and circular does to us. Wittgenstein goes on: 'But I could easily imagine circumstances under which we should say that they had something in common and would not hesitate to say what it was: Imagine a use of language (a culture) in which there was a common name for green and red on the one hand and yellow and blue on the other. Suppose, e.g., that there were two castes, one the patrician caste, wearing red and green garments, the other, the plebian, wearing blue and yellow garments. Both yellow and blue would always be referred to as plebian colours, green and red as patrician colours. Asked what a red patch and a green patch have in common, a man of our tribe would not hesitate to say they were both patrician.'[40]

So Wittgenstein transforms our idea of what makes the grouping of things together arbitrary and what makes it non-arbitrary. If one says that what makes it non-arbitrary is the fact that they have certain properties in common, or that they resemble each other in certain respects, one will be taking for granted what one needs to spell out in philosophy. That is why neither fact can provide the *ultimate* justification of a classification.

Put it like this, classification necessarily presupposes objects, situations, or phenomena, that we can refer to, name and characterise prior to and, therefore, independently of the classification. The similarities and differences that we draw on go with that; they belong with our name for or characterisation of what we classify. We do not classify bare particulars, whatever that may mean; we do not start in a grammatical vacuum. And where we have objects to classify, we have already names for them, and so a whole range of similarities and differences which we can select from in classifying them in different ways. That is we must already have come a long way before we can classify things; we must already have things to classify. So the similarities and differences that hold between what we already call by a certain name cannot give us the basis for our use of that name. Consequently neither can they give us the *ultimate* basis for our use of any word which presupposes its use. Thus if we are to explain what we mean by 'elm tree', we shall point to similarities and differences between trees we call by that name and others we call by other names. But then we would have to go on to explain what makes a plant a tree as opposed to, say, a shrub, and so on. And what we shall come down to *ultimately* will not be, as it were, bare particulars which we call by the same name because of the way they resemble each other, but the *grammar* in which we carry out the comparisons in question.

I have tried to make clear what Wittgenstein's anti-realism in connection with the problem of universals comes to. Both the view that universals are common properties and the view that they are resemblances are forms of realism which Wittgenstein rejects. But the views rejected are not forms of ontology, and neither does Wittgenstein embrace any form of nominalism in rejecting them. With this in mind let us once more return to Quine.

IV. UNIVERSALS AND ONTOLOGY: SOME CONCLUDING REMARKS ON QUINE

Take the following statements:

(a) 'There are cows in the field.'
'There are three even numbers between 3 and 9.'
'There are atoms.'

(b) 'There are universals.'
'There are numbers.'

I have argued that the statements under (a) and under (b) are entirely different in character. Of course, the statements in each category differ among themselves too – despite Quine's claim that these are merely differences in degree. But we are not now concerned with these differences.

Quine, like Moore, thinks that statements in category (a) entail corresponding statements in category (b):
'There are three even numbers between 3 and 9' $\rightarrow$ 'There are numbers'
'This is a hand' $\rightarrow$ 'There are physical objects'

'Tom is just' → 'Justice exists' → 'There are universals'

He speaks of this as 'ontological commitment': 'Ontological statements follow immediately from all manner of casual statements of commonplace fact, just as – from the point of view, anyway, of McX's conceptual scheme – "There is an attribute" follows from "There are red houses, red roses, red sunsets" ' (p. 10).

Quine goes on: 'Judged in another conceptual scheme, an ontological statement which is axiomatic to McX's mind may, with equal immediacy and triviality, be adjudged false. One may admit that there are red houses, roses and sunsets, but deny, except as a popular and misleading manner of speaking, that they have anything in common' (ibid.).

What on Quine's view, I wonder, is our conceptual scheme – I mean that of the plain man? Do the realist and nominalist philosophers, say Locke and Berkeley, have different conceptual schemes? And does the language we speak commit us to a particular philosophy, ontology or metaphysics unless we explicitly dissent from it – as Berkeley may have done when he said that 'we should speak with the vulgar but think with the learned'? Did Berkeley dissent from the commitments of the vulgar tongue which he continued to speak? And is Quine finding fault with the language he speaks, together with us, when he admits that there are red houses, etc., but denies that they have anything in common – except as a popular and misleading manner of speaking?

Well, do they or do they not have anything in common? Does the language we speak commit us to answer this question one way or another? Someone may say: 'If they are all red, they must have something in common, namely that they are all red.' This is what Bambrough characterises as a *platitude*.[41] It is a tautology: 'If they are all red, that is what they all have in common. If they are all red, then they are all red.' Bambrough's platitude is this: 'All things that are correctly called by the same name must have something in common, namely what it is that makes it correct to call them by the same name.' But what is *that*? What is it that makes it correct to call many things by one and the same name? This is the *controversial* question to which the platitude provides no answer. It would not be a platitude if it did. One answer to the controversial question is that all things that are called by the same name must have something in common other than, or over and above, their being of the same kind (e.g. red), over and above their being such that they can all be correctly called by the same name (e.g. 'red'). What they are thus claimed to have in common is meant to explain our grouping them together, our calling them by the same name. On this view, two different things are being claimed: (i) The sunsets, the houses, the roses in question all have something in common, namely that they are red. (ii) They are so by virtue of something else, namely their sharing some one thing, the attribute or essence of redness.

If we collapse (ii) to (i) we get back to our platitude and leave the controversial question unanswered. For it is only by being distinct from (i) that (ii) can provide a basis for (i): 'It is by virtue of sharing the common attribute of redness that all red things are red.' If, on the other hand, the expression 'having the attribute of redness' is used as the equivalent of the expression 'being red', then the above obscure pronouncement becomes a tautology: 'It is by virtue of being red that all red things are red.' Quine confuses the platitudinous with the metaphysical (Platonic) claim: 'For McX there being attributes is even more obvious and trivial than the obvious and trivial fact of their being red houses, roses and sunsets. This, I think, is characteristic of metaphysics, or at least of that part of metaphysics called ontology: one who regards a statement on this subject as true at all must regard it as trivially true' (p. 10). McX regards 'there being attributes' not merely as just as obvious, but as *more* obvious than the obvious fact of there being red houses, roses, and sunsets, because there may not have been any red houses, red roses, and red sunsets, but even then other things would have been red, and if not red then some other colour. As long as we *can* think of or describe anything (as seems incontrovertible), there *must* be some attributes. This is what makes 'There are attributes' so queer a thing to say or think, and what made Wittgenstein remark that 'one might say of logical concepts that their essence proves their existence'.[42]

But is this what McX wishes to assert, and if so why should anyone make any fuss about it? Is this what McX's opponent, the nominalist, wishes to deny when he says that 'red houses, red roses, red sunsets have nothing in common, and to say that they do is to speak misleadingly'? The answer is No, and this is what Quine is unclear about. Surely what he wishes to deny is that it is by virtue of what they share (an attribute, redness) that they are all of the same kind, namely red things. Here 'having an attribute', 'possessing redness' is not meant to be equivalent to 'being red'. It is used to mean 'possessing something which *makes* red things red'. 'It is red by virtue of the redness it has.' This is thought in analogy with: 'It is sweet by virtue of the sugar dissolved in it.' This is the doctrine of *universals as ingredients* which we discussed earlier. It is *this* which McX wishes to assert, and it seems to him 'axiomatic', 'obvious', 'trivially true' because he confuses it with what seems to follow immediately from such 'casual statements of common-place facts' as 'There are red houses, red roses, red sunsets'.

I say 'seems' to follow, because the 'platitude' with which the idea of universals as ingredients is confused, the one expressed by the words 'There are attributes', is no existential statement at all. It says that one *can* describe such things as houses, roses and sunsets by means of colour epithets – in other words that one can intelligibly attribute colours to them, and that one can attribute the same colour to them if they have the same colour in common.

Surely, Quine or the nominalist does not wish to deny *this*. What they wish to deny or combat is the idea of universals as ingredients – the Platonic or the Aristotelian doctrine. Thus Socrates in the *Phaedo*: 'When the Form of Three takes possession of any group of objects, it compels them to be odd as well as three.' 'Whatever [else] is beautiful [apart from absolute Beauty] is beautiful because it partakes of that absolute Beauty and for no other reason.' 'You would loudly proclaim that you know of no other way in which any given object can come into being except by participation in the reality peculiar to its appropriate universal.' This is at least one form of the view which Quine wishes to reject, and it is no platitude, or seeming platitude. It is not anything axiomatic within one conceptual scheme as opposed to another, and one will not get rid of it by modifying the language we speak. In any case, if one could get rid of it that way one would not learn anything from the problem which initiates the manoeuvre. On this Quine is not just confused, but badly confused. His conception of philosophy as science is not just wrong, but shallow. He shows no awareness of the problems, the difficulties from which the views he wishes to oppose come, nor of the depth of these difficulties.

To sum up. Quine says: 'There is not in addition to red things an entity named by redness' (p. 10). 'There is not in addition to just acts and just people an entity named by justice.' I would agree that the word 'justice' is an abstract term and that it does not have meaning by naming an abstract entity. But what does 'abstract entity' mean anyway? Philosophers have talked of 'abstract entities', 'purely intelligible objects' and 'ideal objects' to mean 'something you can think of but not visualise'. The trouble is that 'something you can think of but not visualise' is not a thing, entity or object. This is, I think, part of what Berkeley pointed out when taking issue with Locke over abstract ideas. The view which Quine wishes to reject is that the meaning of general terms is abstract objects or abstract ideas, the essence of the different things which makes them of the same kind and by virtue of which the term applies to them. We have seen what this view amounts to and what is wrong with it. I do not think that Quine sees this. The view in question, we have seen, represents an attempt to base the use or application of words on something more fundamental, a reality that exists independently of language. It could be summed up in two parts: (i) The meaning of a word is an object. (ii) This meaning precedes the word's application and determines it – i.e. the word's application flows from its meaning. Wittgenstein rejects this view and argues that the meaning of a word is to be found in its application or use, and this use or application is exemplified in the appropriate linguistic practices.

Thus the negative philosophical claim that 'There are no universals' or 'There are not abstract objects or entities' is not a negative existential claim like 'There are no unicorns' or 'Dinosaurs have been extinct for a very long time'. Nor, secondly, is it the rejection of a theoretical claim – like 'There is no such thing as phlogiston'. Thus contrast the conflict between the Realist and the Nominalist, discussed in this chapter, with that between Priestley and Lavoisier over whether combustion involves the loss of phlogiston or the gain of oxygen. To see the difference one has to appreciate what is at stake in the two cases and how the two questions are settled. They are very different matters indeed. Nor, thirdly, is the above claim the rejection of a conceptual scheme. It contains no criticism or faulting of the language we speak. The conflict between the Realist and the Nominalist, as I have argued, is neutral with regard to the language we speak.

5 Are there Logical Truths?

I. ANALYTICITY: QUINE'S NEGATIVE THESIS

In 'Two Dogmas of Empiricism' Quine is concerned to combat what he calls 'dogmas of empiricism'. The first of these is the belief that there is 'some fundamental cleavage between truths which are *analytic*, or grounded in meanings independently of matters of fact, and truths which are *synthetic* or grounded in fact'. The second is 'the belief that each meaningful statement is equivalent to some logical construct upon terms which refer to immediate experience' (p. 20). He calls this latter the dogma of reductionism.

In connection with the first Quine examines the notion of analyticity. In connection with the second he examines the notion of verifiability. But, not surprisingly, the notion of verifiability turns out to be central to the second part of the dichotomy of the first 'dogma', namely 'truths that are synthetic or grounded in fact'.

Indeed these two concepts of analyticity and verifiability are central to empiricism and positivism. For empiricism is the view that all knowledge is ultimately based on sense experience and that, therefore, all propositions in which any form of knowledge is expressed are ultimately verifiable by sense experience. Positivism is the view that any proposition which purports to assert anything that goes beyond what experience warrants cannot make sense and does not state anything intelligible. Secondly, the notion of analyticity is crucial to maintaining this position. For it enables philosophers to provide an account of mathematical and logical propositions consistent with empiricism. The truth of such propositions, one wishes to say, is recognised without recourse to empirical investigation. The empiricist who wishes to hold that there can be no a priori knowledge of nature, that reason alone cannot provide any new knowledge of nature, claims that mathematical and logical propositions are true solely by virtue of the meanings of their terms. That is they are not true by virtue of any facts that transcend sense experience and are accessible to the faculty of reason. This is what they are getting at when they characterise such propositions as analytic.

Quine argues that both these notions are defective and that there are no propositions that are true *solely* by virtue of the meanings of their terms. These are certainly relevant to the truth of *all* propositions; but more than this is relevant to the truth not only of what has been characterised as synthetic propositions, but *also* to the truth of logical and mathematical propositions.

So far so good; I should not wish to disagree with Quine. I do not think that the notion of analyticity provides a satisfactory account of logical and mathematical propositions. But to criticise and reject that account is not to reject the contrast between empirical and logical or mathematical propositions.

Secondly, it may of course be that the line between propositions which we regard as necessarily true and those which we regard as contingently true is not a sharp one and that there are propositions which fall in between. It may be that we cannot characterise them as one or the other without qualification.[1] It may be, too, that where we can draw a line, this line is not immutable. But this does not mean that we should abandon the distinction between necessary and contingent truth.

Thirdly, one may agree that what we call arithmetic is not as such necessary – as Plato thought it was. But it does not follow from this that there are no necessities *within* mathematics. Again, one may agree with Wittgenstein that the necessities within mathematics cannot be divorced from the application of mathematics and, therefore, from that *outside* mathematics which gives point to its application.[2] But this interdependence between mathematical propositions and non-mathematical propositions in which mathematics finds an application does not imply that mathematical propositions are not necessarily true, true come what may.

I would, therefore, argue that, whatever the correct account of logical necessity and contingent truth, we have here an important distinction. But does Quine reject it?

I think he does, although some of the words in which he expresses it are not entirely unequivocal. Take his words, 'there is no fundamental cleavage . . .'. If this means, 'there is no absolute cleavage', i.e. that there is no sharp line, then what he says would be less radical than he intends it to be. Similarly, if he means that the dividing line is not immutable. Quine expresses the dichotomy he wishes to reject in terms of the analytic/synthetic distinction. But these words were used by positivists to provide an *account* of the dichotomy. To reject the account is not the same thing as rejecting the dichotomy itself, and it need not amount to such a rejection. After all for Kant the analytic/synthetic distinction did not coincide with the a priori/a posteriori distinction. In the latter Kant was distinguishing between propositions that are true and can be known to be true independently of experience or sense perception, such as mathematical propositions, and those whose truth depends on what could be otherwise and, therefore, cannot be recognised independently of a consideration of contingent matters. He argued that the former propositions are not all analytic, that some of them are synthetic. To argue, as Quine does, that we cannot provide a non-circular definition of analyticity, and so a satisfactory way of drawing the distinction which the analytic/synthetic dichotomy purports to provide, is not *that far* to deny the reality of the a priori/a posteriori distinction.

Quine, however, does wish to deny the reality of the latter distinction. He argued that there is no qualitative difference between geometry and physics, for instance, that the difference between them is one of degree, not of kind, and that in the last resort there is no difference between the way the truth of a geometrical proposition is established and the way the truth of a proposition of physics is established. His view is that in both cases our grounds are ultimately pragmatic.

In fact, broadly, Quine's paper divides into two parts. (i) In the first he argues that, contrary to appearances, the notion of analyticity cannot be defined or explained without circularity. He argues that attempts to define it have been in terms of other concepts, such as 'self-contradiction', 'necessity', 'synonymy', 'semantic rule', which are themselves just as much in need of definition. Each is defined in terms of the others, and no definition breaks out of this circle. (ii) In the second part of his paper he argues that no proposition is immune from revision as such, unassailable or unretractable, and that it is on pragmatic grounds that we choose to regard certain propositions as true come what may and refuse to give them up. It is, therefore, open to us to regard *any* proposition in this way, to give it the status of incontestability. In other words, there are no propositions which cannot be rejected in principle in the light of further experience, none that we are forced to regard as unassailable. Hence no proposition is intrinsically incorrigible. That is it is not by virtue of its structure that a proposition is either immune from revision in the light of experience (i.e. true a priori, necessarily true) or verifiable by it, open to confirmation and disconfirmation. 'By virtue of its structure': This is an expression which Wittgenstein uses in the *Tractatus*. Quine does not. He would say 'singly', or 'intrinsically', or 'in isolation from other propositions'.

My immediate comment on this second thesis is that it contains much to which I am sympathetic. I would agree that those who said that a proposition is necessarily true is so by virtue of its analyticity were wrong and barking up the wrong tree. But to say that no proposition is, in isolation or by virtue of its structure, immune from revision is not to say that no proposition is immune from revision or necessarily true.

Let me begin by summarising Quine's criticism of the notion of analyticity. I have already pointed out that the reason why empiricists have characterised necessary truths as analytic was because they wanted to avoid (i) the idea that there are necessary connections in nature or *de re* necessities, and (ii) the idea that we can have knowledge of nature a priori. But what makes a proposition analytic?

Quine asks this question and points out difficulties which he claims are insuperable. The main one he underlines is that the notion of analyticity cannot be defined or explained without circularity, and that it is based on a presupposition that is incoherent. First about the circularity.

Quine begins by pointing out that the analytic/synthetic dichotomy is to be found in Hume, Leibniz and Kant. In Leibniz it takes the form of a distinction between truths of reason and truths of fact, the former explained as truths that hold in all possible worlds, in other words truths that cannot be denied without self-contradiction. Quine points out that this explanation does not further our understanding since the notion of self-contradiction is itself in need of clarification.

Kant's explanation of what an analytic proposition is fares no better. For what Kant claimed is that an analytic proposition is one whose predicate is contained in its subject. But not all propositions are of the S–P kind – mathematical propositions like 7 + 5 = 12 (Kant's example) are not. Besides, the notion of inclusion or containment used by Kant is metaphorical, and it is doubtful that it can be made clear and precise. Quine says, however, that Kant's intention was clear and that by an analytic proposition he meant one that is 'true by virtue of meanings and independently of fact' (p. 21). The trouble is, Quine argues, that the notion of meaning is in need of clarification. As in his former paper, 'On What there is', Quine suggests that we would be well advised to avoid this notion and instead to speak of the synonymy of linguistic expressions.

Quine argues that this notion is fundamental to the notion of analyticity, though it is itself in need of clarification. How is it fundamental? Quine says that by general philosophical consent there are two kinds of proposition that are analytic:

1.   No unmarried man is married.
2.   No bachelor is married.

It is the second that is problematic, and until the sense in which it is analytic can be clarified the notion of analyticity will not have been clarified.

Quine characterises the first proposition as a 'logical truth'. It is true by virtue of its form, by virtue solely of the logical particles which figure among its components: 'No x that is unϕ is a ϕx.' To characterise the second proposition as analytic is to claim that it can be turned into the first, i.e. reduced to a logical truth, by 'putting synonyms for synonyms' (p. 23).

From this point onwards Quine embarks on a search for the clarification of the notion of synonymy of linguistic expressions. First (in §2) he asks whether the notion of a definition is of any help: 'Two linguistic expressions are synonymous if they have the same definition.' Quine argues that this is putting the cart before the horse. For what is a lexicographer's definition founded on? It is founded on an observed synonymy. It cannot therefore be taken as the ground for the synonymy (p. 24). Quine then considers philosophical and explicative definition, and concludes that 'in formal and informal works alike . . . definition – except in the extreme case of the explicitly conventional introduction of new notations – hinges on prior relations of synonymy' (p. 27). Hence it cannot be used to clarify the notion of synonymy; to attempt to do so would be going round in a circle.

What about the interchangeability of linguistic expressions? Quine asks (in §3) whether this notion is of any help: 'Two linguistic expressions are synonymous if they can be interchanged in all contexts without changing the truth-value of the propositions in which they are used – interchangeable *salva veritate*.' Is this a strong enough or sufficient condition for synonymy? At first it seems that it is: 'we can quickly assure ourselves that it is (Quine says) by examples of the following sort' (p. 29). Take the proposition:

(A)   Necessarily all and only all bachelors are bachelors

This, Quine claims, is evidently true. (I do not, myself, understand what these words are meant to assert, and I doubt that anyone else does. But I shall let that pass.)

If 'bachelor' and 'unmarried man' are interchangeable s.v., then the proposition we get by substituting 'unmarried man' for 'bachelor', namely,

(B)   Necessarily all and only bachelors are unmarried men

must be true, since the truth-value of the first proposition is not affected by the interchange.

But to say 'Necessarily p is true' is to say that 'p is analytic'.

And if p, namely 'All and only bachelors are unmarried men', is analytic, then 'bachelor' and 'unmarried man' are synonymous.

For to say that 'bachelor' and 'unmarried man' are synonymous *is* to say that the proposition 'All and only bachelors are unmarried men' is analytic.

The trouble, as Quine points out, is that we have assumed here the notion of analyticity in explaining the notion of synonymy, and so we have gone round in a circle again. He concludes that 'if a language contains an intensional adverb "necessarily" . . ., or other particles to the same effect, then interchangeability s.v. in such a language does afford a sufficient condition of [cognitive] synonymy; but such a language is intelligible only insofar as the notion of analyticity is already understood in advance' (p. 31).

Next, and thirdly, Quine asks (in §4) whether an appeal to semantical rules would help to clarify the notion of analyticity: 'A proposition is analytic if it is not merely true but true according to a semantical rule.' But the notion of semantical rule is in need of clarification. How are the semantical rules of a language to be distinguished from the analytic propositions the analyticity of which they are supposed to depend on? The discussion of this question leads Quine to the conclusion that 'semantical rules determining the analytic statements of an artificial language are of interest only insofar as we already understand the notion of analyticity, they are of no help in gaining this understanding' (p. 36).

Then, fourthly, Quine turns to the verification theory of meaning (in §5). Can the notion of verification or confirmation by experience help to throw light on the notion of analyticity – either by contrast or indirectly by clarifying the notion of synonymy? By contrast: 'A synthetic proposition is one that can be verified or falsified by experience. An analytic proposition is the limiting case where the proposition is true come what may – "confirmed no matter what" – or, which comes to the same thing, where no experience can falsify or disconfirm it.' Compare with Wittgenstein's representation of a tautology in the *Tractatus*, 'TTTT . . . (p,q, . . .)', as a degenerate truth-function (4.466). Indirectly, through its definition of propositional synonymy: 'Two propositions are synonymous if they have the same method of verification.' If this can be accepted, says Quine, as an adequate account of statement-synonymy, the notion of analyticity would be saved: 'For (then) a statement may be described as analytic simply when it is synonymous with a logically true statement' (p. 38). But can it be accepted? 'Just what are these methods which are to be compared for likeness?' (ibid.)

The conclusion which Quine comes to is that the experiences which are supposed to confront our statements or propositions, thus verifying or falsifying them, do not confront these individually, but 'only as a corporate body' (p. 41). Hence there are no methods of verification which can help us identify individual propositions as synonymous with each other.

In this way Quine takes himself (i) to have established the negative thesis that the notion of analyticity cannot be defined without circularity, and (ii) to have reached the point from which he can go ahead and develop his positive theses that no proposition is intrinsically unassailable – or, if I may deliberately put it another way, that there is nothing in any proposition we regard as necessarily true to make it necessarily true. The link between the positive and the negative theses is that analyticity has been widely regarded by empiricists as precisely that in or about a proposition which makes it necessarily true. This is a contingent, or historical, link, one which rests on certain philosophical presuppositions. If, however, one is oneself wedded to the idea that analyticity is the only thing about a proposition which can make it necessarily true, if anything can, if one sees no other account of logical necessity compatible with empiricism, then when one comes to see that view to be defective one may feel one is confronted with a dilemma: *Either* one has to give up empiricism and admit that there are necessities *de re, or* one has to give up the idea of logical necessity altogether. Quine is wedded to this idea. So when he can no longer hold on to the view that necessary truths are analytic, he cannot hold on to the view that there are necessary truths, i.e. to the possibility of distinguishing between necessary and contingent truths.

It is possible to look at this conclusion differently and see there, not the rejection of logical necessity, but the introduction of an alternative account of logical necessity – one that has certain affinities with Conventionalism and Pragmatism. Quine does not see it this way however. He would probably say: 'Nothing that accords with such an account (i.e. with conventionalism and pragmatism) deserves to be characterised as ''logically necessary'' or as ''necessarily true''.' I should not blame him for thinking so. For if Quine's positive thesis is to be taken as an account of logical necessity, it has to be admitted that it is a defective account, although by no means one that is devoid of interest. As a matter of fact, I think that it is in some ways like the account we can extract from Wittgenstein's discussion of logical necessity, though it is an altogether cruder account. And it is defective in just those respects in which it differs from Wittgenstein's account, namely in its conventionalism, pragmatism, and positivism – despite Quine's criticism of 'the dogma of reductionism'.

While I think that it is important to clarify the notion of analyticity and to criticise the empiricist view that necessary truths are analytic and that it is this that makes them necessary, I cannot get very excited by Quine's formal conclusion that we cannot define analyticity without circularity, nor by the way he goes about establishing it. Thus compare the view that all necessary truths are analytic with Wittgenstein's view in the *Tractatus* that all logical propositions are tautologies and that we recognise them from the symbol alone. Also compare Quine's criticism of the analytic view with Wittgenstein's criticism of the *Tractatus* view developed from 1929 onwards. Wittgenstein's critique has both a much wider focus and is also the deeper of the two critiques.

Wittgenstein's critique of the view of logic in the *Tractatus* took its start from reflections on colour-incompatibility and propositions which attribute qualities to things which admit of degrees. The realisation which these reflections brought to him was that the logical constants 'and', 'or', 'if . . . then', etc. have a wider logic than he had recognised in the *Tractatus*, and that there are many valid inferrential forms which cannot be represented as tautologies. This was a first step, but a fundamental one, towards a conception of logic, and therefore of inference, logical truth and necessity, radically different from the views developed in the *Tractatus*, but it did not go back on the contrast he had made in the *Tractatus*, within the framework of truth-functional logic, between logic and empirical science – between propositions which he expresses as 'TTTT . . . (p,q, . . .)', characterised as propositions 'devoid of sense', and propositions which are falsifiable, 'TTFT . . . (p,q, . . .)'. He had said that 'all theories that make a proposition of logic appear to have content are false' (6.111). He never went back on this, and later referred to what he rejected as a view of logic which turns it into a supra-physics. The radical shift in his view of logic consists in his reversal of the relation between logic and language. As Rhees puts it: 'That idea of "the logical structure of language" would illustrate what he

(Wittgenstein) would now call a *misunderstanding* of the logic of language. The whole idea of a structure or system, like the idea of a logical connection, depends on what speaking is.'[3]

The idea is not that we cannot speak of the logical structure of proposition or of the rules of syntax that govern logical inferences, but that these are what appear in the employment of propositions, of language, in the course of conversations, discussions, investigations and reasonings in the weave of our lives.[4] They are not something that can be identified a priori and in abstraction from what we actually do with language in our lives. They do not, therefore, constitute anything more fundamental than what we actually do, and they bring in the circumstances of our lives.

In his criticism of the notion of analyticity and his movement towards pragmatism Quine too is moving away from some of the ideas which Wittgenstein was criticising, even though he does not move in the same direction. In one respect he does not go as far as Wittgenstein, while in another respect he goes further and, indeed, too far. The respect in which he does not go far enough is his 'formalism', i.e. his abstract treatment of language – so that, for instance, he can speak of the statement 'Necessarily all and only bachelors are bachelors' as 'evidently true'. This has been characterised by Wittgenstein as 'looking at language without looking at the language-game'. The respect in which he goes too far is to be found in his rejection of the distinction between logical and empirical truth.

Indeed his criticism of the notion of analyticity leading to the conclusion that it cannot be defined without circularity – both his procedure and his conclusion are too 'formalistic' by half. I think that Professors Strawson and Grice in their paper 'In Defence of a Dogma'[5] bring this out well. They say, quite rightly, that Quine's negative thesis is concerned not simply with analyticity, but with a whole family of logical notions, including those of self-contradiction, logical necessity, synonymy, claiming that our understanding of any one of them involves an understanding of the others, so that none can be explained without taking some of the others as already understood. Consequently there cannot be an explanation that does not in part take for granted or presuppose the very understanding it aims at imparting. This is not, of course, surprising and is intimately connected with the reason why Wittgenstein, in the *Tractatus*, distinguished between what can be said and what cannot be said but shows itself in the language we use.[6] From the impossibility of such an explanation, however, it does not follow that the notions in question are unclear, nor that there is nothing that philosophy can do to throw light on them insofar as they give rise to philosophical difficulties.

As Strawson and Grice point out, perhaps these notions cannot be explained formally in the way Quine requires. But this does not mean that they cannot be explained at all. They can be, though less formally. Strawson and Grice provide such an informal explanation of the notion of logical impossibility by means of an imaginary example. The explanation they give, they point out, breaks out of the family circle. The distinction in which this explanation ultimately comes to rest is that between 'not believing something' and 'not understanding something'. They say: 'It would be rash to maintain that *this* distinction does not need clarification; but it would be absurd to maintain that it does not exist.' Their suggestion is that Quine's formal requirement comes from confusion and that the fact that it cannot be fulfilled is, therefore, no ground for commiseration: 'The expressions which belong to the circle have an intelligible use and mark genuine distinctions.' They mean such distinctions as between self-contradiction and falsity, logical necessity and contingency, synonymy and heteronomy, not believing something and not understanding something.

It seems to me that the question of how best to understand these distinctions, say that between necessary truth and contingent truth, and whether we can do so in terms of the concept of analyticity, has only been answered negatively in this sense: We do not have an independent understanding of analyticity, we do not understand it independently of what it is supposed to help us understand better, namely the notion of necessary truth. Therefore, it cannot increase our understanding of the latter notion.

This is true. But it fails to show much appreciation of the kind of understanding we lack and, therefore, seek in philosophy. When we ask, 'What is logical necessity? How does a necessary truth differ from a contingent one?', we are already familiar with the distinction in question. If we were not, we could not ask the question, nor could we know what would constitute a satisfactory answer to it. We are not like someone doing research in medicine who asks 'What is cancer?' We are asking for an 'elucidation'[7] of what we already know.[8] Hence the fact that we cannot have an altogether independent understanding of the terms in which we give our elucidations does not disqualify them from their elucidatory role. On the contrary, if we could have had an altogether independent understanding of them they would only succeed in providing a distorted account and not an elucidation. We can find plenty of examples of this in ethics – e.g. the analysis of moral concepts in terms of self-interest – and in other branches of philosophy.

Can we understand the notion of logical necessity in terms of analyticity? What Quine brings out in the first part of his discussion, that is his negative claim that this notion cannot be defined without presupposing an understanding of what it is intended to elucidate, does not provide a negative answer to the above question. That far, for all Quine's impressive undertaking, that question remains unanswered. In other words, if an account of logical necessity in terms of analyticity is unsatisfactory, as I believe it is, this is not because that notion cannot be defined without circularity.

Quine's negative answer to the above question, towards which I am sympathetic, has an independent support. This emerges in the last part of his discussion in that paper. This is now what I turn to.

II. LOGICAL NECESSITY: QUINE'S POSITIVE THESIS

One could state Quine's positive thesis as follows:

1. It is an illusion to suppose that there is any class of accepted propositions the members of which are in principle unfalsifiable, unassailable, true a priori, necessarily true. It is an illusion to think that it is by virtue of what they are in themselves, by virtue of some logical structure inherent in the symbol, that propositions which express logical truths are necessarily true, immune from falsification, true come what may.

2. Propositions which admit of confirmation and disconfirmation and purport to express contingent truths 'face the tribunal of sense experience not individually but only as a corporate body' (p. 41).

These are two sides of the same coin. In the rest of this chapter I shall be concerned with the first part of Quine's positive thesis. I shall return to the second part in the next chapter. Take first the first part of Quine's thesis:

No proposition is (absolutely) immune from revision or unfalsifiable.

And to this a minor premise:

A necessary truth, or a proposition which is necessarily true, is one which is (absolutely) immune from revision or unfalsifiable.

And the conclusion follows:

There are no propositions that are necessarily true.

This conclusion contradicts the claim:

Some propositions are necessarily true in contrast to others that are contingently true and, therefore, falsifiable.

This is another way of saying:

There is a distinction to be made between one kind of proposition and another according to whether the truth of a proposition is logically necessary or contingent.

And this is precisely the first of Quine's 'two dogmas of empiricism'.

This argument for the rejection of Quine's first 'dogma' of empiricism is entirely independent of his argument against the possibility of a non-circular explanation, or formal definition of analyticity.

Let us begin by considering the major premise first: No proposition is (absolutely) immune from revision or unfalsifiable. Quine arrives at it through a criticism of the verification theory and his rejection of an idea central to it, namely Quine's second dogma of empiricism: 'the dogma of reductionism'. According to the verification theory a proposition is true if it is verified by experience and false if it is falsified. But if it is a genuine proposition, if it really says anything, it must in principle be capable of verification. To understand it, to grasp what it claims, i.e. its meaning, is to know *what* would verify it. By 'knowing its method of verification' Logical Positivists meant 'knowing the sorts of experience that would verify it and so knowing in what direction to look, where to seek its confirmation'. Whatever shows that one knows this shows that one knows the meaning of the proposition, that one understands what it says.

How would one describe what verifies a proposition? Presumably one would describe the experiences which would verify it. But that description would itself be a proposition or set of propositions. These, in turn, if they are intelligible, would have to have a method of verification. So Logical Positivists had to face two problems: (i) Regarding the propositions which give the original proposition's method of verification and, therefore, its meaning: How are *they* related to experience? (ii) Regarding the relation between the proposition in question and those propositions (sometimes referred to as 'protocol sentences') which set out its verification: If they give the meaning of the proposition must they not entail the proposition? Must the proposition not be a translation of the protocol sentences which give it its meaning?

Quine's critique here is directed at the idea that language confronts experience through individual propositions which are its units of meaning. Frege, Russell, and Wittgenstein in the *Tractatus* had argued that words or names do not have meaning individually and on their own. Now Quine sees himself as making a similar claim for sentences or propositions: 'The idea of defining a symbol in use was . . . an advance over the impossible term-by-term empiricism of Locke and Hume. The statement, rather than the term, came with Bentham to be recognised as the unit accountable to an empiricist critique. But what I am now urging is that even in taking the statement as unit we have drawn our grid too finely. The unit of empirical significance is the whole of science' (p. 42).

Quine thus goes on to argue that the propositions which we enunciate in language, the things that we claim to know or believe, form a *system* – they constitute 'a man-made fabric' (p. 42). These include propositions about the most casual of matters as well as those in which we state 'the profoundest laws of atomic physics or even of pure mathematics and logic'. When we have an experience or make an observation relevant to the truth of any proposition we are never forced to accept the proposition as true, just as when we have an experience or make an observation relevant to the truth of its contradictory we are not forced to reject it as false. It is always open to us not to accept it, or not to reject it, by revising our view of the truth-value of other propositions.

This view is, I think, most convincing in science where two radically opposed theories are put to the test and, therefore, best illustrated in that context. One could put it there by saying that there are no crucial experiments, that is experiments that would definitively establish or finally overthrow a theory, that a theory has to prove its worth over a longer period.[9] To say this is not to reject or express scepticism about the experimental method in physics and chemistry, but to comment on the way it works.

Let us, as an example, consider briefly the conflict between Lavoisier and Priestley, towards the end of the eighteenth century, about whether combustion consists of the gain of oxygen by or the loss of phlogiston from combustible substances.

Lavoisier heated some mercury of a given weight in a furnace connected to a closed quantity of air of known volume. After this process of heating went on for a certain length of time, he found that the mercury was covered by small red particles adding to its total weight, while the air had decreased by one sixth of its volume and had become 'azotic', that is no longer fit for respiration or combustion – animals submerged in it suffocated, and a taper plunged into it went out. He then reversed the experiment and found these results reversed.

Bearing in mind the principle of the conservation of mass Lavoisier concluded: (i) The conversion of grains of calx to mercury (when the experiment was reversed) produced the release of respirable air in a quantity equal to the loss of volume when the mercury originally turned into calx. So the calx must have formed as a result of mercury taking up or uniting with respirable air from the closed jar – not as a result of losing phlogiston. (ii) The calcination stopped when all the respirable portion of the air in the closed jar had been used up. (iii) He further concluded that atmospheric air is composed of two gases, respirable and mephistic or azotic, and not, as Priestley had supposed, of one substance with two states, saturated with and deprived of phlogiston. The respirable part was a specific gas with a base of oxygen whose participation is indispensable for combustion, respiration and calcination, or as we now call it oxydisation.

Commenting on this experiment in their book *The Architecture of Matter* Toulmin and Goodfield observe:

> To modern ideas, indeed, it has sometimes appeared as though this experiment destroys single-handed the whole basis of the phlogiston theory. First, the calx is produced from mercury, and the air loses one sixth of its volume; then, mercury is recovered from the calx (HgO), and a corresponding volume of respirable air appears. As we watch the volumes of gas changing we seem to see irresistible proof that the calx is a compound – produced from the metal by imbibing respirable air . . . – the evidence of the scales only confirming what our sight has already told us . . . But . . . what we 'see' happening is read into the experiment by our theoretical hindsight . . . Other eighteenth century chemists watching the experiment for the first time 'saw' it very differently (p. 226).

In 1783 Priestley devised a rival experiment. He put a quantity of lead calx in a crucible which he placed on a stand and he introduced it into a large receiver filled with inflammable air (hydrogen). Then he heated it with a burning glass. When the calx was dry, it became black and turned into lead. At the same time the inflammable air diminished and the water in which the large receiver was inverted for isolation from the surrounding air rose. He concluded that obviously the calx was imbibing something from the air which turned the calx into metal and that this substance being imbibed by the calx was phlogiston.

Again Toulmin and Goodfield comment:

> In point of logic, it is hard to find fault with Priestley's conclusion. In point of vividness, his demonstration was (if anything) *more* convincing than Lavoisier's. For the air in Lavoisier's bell-jar lost only one sixth of its volume when the metallic mercury turned to red calx, whereas in Priestley's counter-demonstration, when the lead calx turned to metallic lead, *all* the hydrogen in the container disappeared.
>
> How unfortunate – we may be tempted to reply – that Priestley enclosed his hydrogen over *water*. As we now interpret it, the heated calx gave off oxygen, which combined with the hydrogen in the jar to form a minute extra quantity of water: thus the illusion was produced that the calx and the hydrogen

(evidently rich in phlogiston) had combined to form lead. If Priestley had noticed the extra water, could he have drawn the conclusion he did? He could and he did . . . The water, he argued, was only a by-product of the reaction: the basic phenomenon was still the union of the calx with phlogiston from the hydrogen to form the metal.

On the basis of the rival demonstrations *alone*, Priestley was entitled to hold his ground. For where we nowadays 'see' oxygen being evolved from heated mercury calx, Priestley 'saw' – even more vividly – hydrogen being imbibed by heated lead calx. And the true lesson to be learned from comparing their demonstrations is, in fact, this: that an overall reordering of chemical theory such as Lavoisier had proposed *could not* stand or fall by a single observation, or depend for its justification on any one 'crucial experiment' . . . It was the *systematic* character of Lavoisier's theory – its power to embrace more and more chemical reactions, with the minimum of arbitrary assumptions – that ultimately carried weight with his colleagues. The phlogiston theory, by contrast, remained arbitrary and unsystematic, having to be trimmed and adjusted afresh to meet the demands of each new phenomenon, and this was a good sign that something was amiss with its principles. Indeed, Lavoisier's main complaint against the phlogiston theory was not that it *mis*represented Nature, but that it failed to give any clear representation of Nature at all (pp. 226–8).

Quine wishes to generalise this to the confirmation and disconfirmation of *any* proposition whatever. Whenever we consider a proposition to be confirmed or disconfirmed we make, implicitly, a great many assumptions. That is we regard other propositions as true. To claim that experience confirms or disconfirms proposition p is to claim that such-and-such experiences obtain *and* that q, r, s and t are true. Experience can never confirm or disconfirm any single proposition in isolation. No experience can *force* me to retract or revise an individual proposition p, except in conjunction with other propositions q, r, s and t. I can retract p in the face of the experience (or despite it) by giving up some of these propositions. And I can do so, give up r and s for instance, because equally no experience can force me to accept r and s. It is only because I hold on to q, r, s and t that some experience obliges me to declare that p is false. This is what

Quine means when he says that 'our statements about the external world face the tribunal of sense experience not individually but only as a corporate body'. So, Quine's view is, when I hold that p is true, it is never on the basis of experience *alone* that I do so. It is on the basis of experience *plus* the fact that I accept certain other propositions, make certain assumptions. But what does 'experience' mean in this context? How do we identify particular experiences, if not through individual propositions? I shall return to these questions in the last chapter when I consider what Quine has to say on what he calls 'observation sentences'. In short, then, on Quine's view, I can never be forced to accept any proposition as true no matter what happens because I always have a way out, I have always an alternative to accepting it as true. The question of whether or not I take such a way out, what alternative I go along with, is a pragmatic question.

Now for propositions which we regard as necessarily true or unassailable. Quine holds that it cannot be claimed that we do so because of anything intrinsic to the symbol in which such propositions are expressed, such as their logical structure, or the meanings alone of the words in which they are expressed. While I go along with this, I do not see that Quine has shown us why. He holds that we regard them as necessarily true because we are unwilling to give them up under forseeable conditions. They are unassailable or immune from falsification because, no matter how unfavourable to their truth any experience may be, we hold on to them by giving up some other proposition we may have regarded as true in the way just explained. It is not a matter of what the symbol imposes on us, but of our choice, informed by pragmatic considerations.

Quine holds that this cannot be a matter of logical necessity because there is nothing in the symbol to force us, because our hands are not tied, and because he does not see any qualitative difference between such propositions and those which are vulnerable to falsification. Those that are vulnerable to falsification are so because we refuse to admit others to be false. Similarly, those that are invulnerable are so because we allow others to be falsified under certain circumstances. There is no intrinsic difference between the former and the latter ones. It is on pragmatic grounds that we regard certain propositions as invulnerable; which we so regard is determined by pragmatic considerations. It is always conceivable that circumstances may make it advisable for us to re-draw the line between these two groups. As Quine puts it: 'Total science is like a field of force whose boundary conditions are experience. A conflict with experience at the periphery occasions readjustments in the interior of the field. Truth values have to be redistributed over some of our statements. Re-evaluation of some statements entails re-evaluation of others, because of their logical interconnections – the logical laws being in turn certain further statements of the system, certain further elements of the field' (p. 42).

Quine here speaks of a 'system' of propositions and of the 'logical interconnections' between propositions that are members of the system. At the same time he speaks of logical propositions or laws as being members of the system. Now a system involves logical ordering, logical interconnections between its members, and presumably logical propositions give expression to the order and interconnections that constitute the system. In that case how can logical propositions themselves be members of the system? It seems to me that Quine is confusing the representations we make in language of the things we talk about and our mode of representation – the method we employ in representing the things we talk about. And to say that there is no logical necessity about what method we use in representing the things we talk about is not to deny the above distinction – a point to which I shall return.

Quine continues:

The total field is so underdetermined by its boundary conditions, experience, that there is much latitude of choice as to what statements to re-evaluate in the light of any single contrary experience. No particular experiences are linked with any particular statements in the interior of the field, except indirectly through considerations of equilibrium affecting the field as a whole.

If this view is right, it is misleading to speak of the empirical content of an individual statement – especially if it is a statement at all remote from the experiential periphery of the field. Furthermore it becomes folly to seek a boundary between synthetic statements, which hold contingently on experience, and analytic statements, which hold come what may. Any statement can be held true come what may, if we make drastic enough adjustments elsewhere in the system . . . Conversely, by the same token, no statement is immune to revision (pp. 42–3).

Earlier I had set out Quine's argument for the conclusion that the distinction between necessary and contingent truths is spurious as follows:

No proposition is (absolutely) immune from revision or unfalsifiable.

A necessary truth, i.e. a proposition which is necessarily true, is one which is (absolutely) immune from revision or unfalsifiable.

Therefore, there are no propositions that are necessarily true or unfalsifiable.

We have seen something of Quine's reasons for holding to what I have represented as the major premise of the above argument, and so something of what it comes to. We shall have to return to it and criticise it. I think that in it truth and falsity are intermingled and will have to be disentangled.

In connection with the minor premise I hope to show that what Quine requires from a proposition before he can agree to regard it as expressing a necessary truth is confused. I shall do so through a brief consideration of Wittgenstein's discussion of logical necessity.

Once this is seen it will be evident, I hope, that there are no good grounds for the conclusion that there are no propositions which are necessarily true or unfalsifiable, and so no distinction to be made between necessary and contingent truth.

III. STRAWSON AND GRICE ON QUINE'S POSITIVE THESIS

Strawson and Grice argue that Quine's positive thesis is not incompatible with the distinction which Quine wishes to reject as spurious or a dogma:

1.   Quine holds that no proposition is in principle immune from revision in the light of experience. In other words, any

proposition, including those we regard as necessarily true, may be given up, provided we are prepared to make adjustments for doing so and find it convenient to do so. Strawson and Grice argue that one can agree with this and go on to distinguish between two different kinds of giving up – between the kind of giving up which consists in merely admitting falsity and the kind of giving up which involves change in our concepts. In the latter case, I am inclined to say, what we are giving up is not a truth but a particular concept-formation. I shall return to this point.

2.   Quine holds that what we have to renounce in the light of experience is determined by what we are anxious to keep. But then there is a distinction between what we regard as falsifiable and what we regard as immune from falsification. The fact that what we regard as immune from falsification is something which we may come to regard as falsifiable does not mean that it was not so regarded, nor, while it was so regarded, that it was not genuinely immune from falsification. Nor does this imply that we can speak and reason without regarding some propositions as immune from falsification. Hence the distinction which Quine rejects has not been shown by him to be spurious.

3.   Quine thinks, I think quite rightly, that there is no absolute necessity about the adoption of any conceptual scheme – or, as Wittgenstein would put it, no logical necessity about the adoption of any concept-formation. But it does not follow from this that there are no necessities *within* the conceptual scheme or concept-formation. Wittgenstein expressed this by saying that a mathematical proof does not compel us to accept its conclusion, it does not force us to go along with it. It merely 'persuades' us, 'guides' us towards a particular concept-formation. But then he distinguished this kind of proof which extends our mathematics from the kind of calculation *within* our established mathematics where a conclusion follows from the premises with logical necessity. He then went on to ask what this necessity amounts to and where its source lies.

4.   There may well be propositions which we are inclined to assert, many such to be found in the pages of philosophy books, over the acceptance of which we may be in conflict, or which we may feel we cannot accept while saying that if such a proposition is true then it is necessarily true. Equally, a form of words may express at one go more than one proposition, and some of these may express a necessary truth or falsity. Strawson, Grice, and

also Waismann, think that it may be pointless to press the question whether such a form of words express a necessary or contingent truth. Sometimes this is so, and sometimes pressing the question may force us to distinguish between the different propositions expressed by the form of words in question.[10]

5.　Strawson and Grice reply to Quine's criticism of the view that two propositions are synonymous if they have the same verification. Quine had argued that no proposition is verified by experience except on the assumption that a number of other propositions are true. But then, Strawson and Grice reply, we can compare two propositions with regard to their verification provided that we ensure that these other propositions assumed to be true are the same in the two cases. When this is so, then two propositions which have the same verification may, with justification, be regarded as synonymous. As they put it: 'Acceptance of Quine's doctrine of empirical confirmation does not, as he says it does, entail giving up the attempt to define statement-synonymy in terms of confirmation.'

IV.　WITTGENSTEIN ON LOGICAL NECESSITY: IS IT A FORM OF COMPULSION?

Wittgenstein would have agreed that a consideration of the symbol or the structure of a proposition will not get us very far in the clarification of the notion of logical necessity. This is not to deny that there is an intimate connection between the meaning of the terms of a proposition, the sense of the proposition, and its logical relations. There is, and in fact these are the two sides of the same coin. But they are on the same level. Therefore the logical implications of a proposition cannot be said to depend on or flow from its sense. Similarly for a proposition which expresses a logical truth: We cannot say that its truth or necessity derives from its sense.

The trouble is that when we think this it seems that the sense of a proposition or the meanings of logical constants are some kind of ethereal rails along which our thoughts must flow, so that we are compelled to accept the proposition or make the deduction. Wittgenstein criticises this idea. He points out that it comes from confusions about what it is for words and propositions to have meaning. But to reject it, to claim that 'there is no logical compulsion', is not to reject the notion of logical necessity. Any more than rejecting the idea of the essence of a kind is to reject the generality implicit in the meaning of our name for that kind, and so to embrace some form of nominalism. It is only if one cannot separate the idea criticised from the notion of logical necessity that one will think that a criticism of the former constitutes an attack on the latter. This is true of Quine. Hence the minor premise of the argument I attributed to him.

'There is no logical compulsion.' Wittgenstein uses words to this effect in two different connections. First, in connection with drawing a logical inference, arriving at a conclusion by calculation. What he says is meant to apply to the inference and calculation, and equally to the principles of inference, the mathematical propositions in accordance with which transitions are made in the course of the calculation. More generally, it is meant to apply to what he calls 'rules of grammar' or 'rules of the language-game'. In other words, Wittgenstein uses the above words in connection with logical steps that have become established, steps which we all accept unquestioningly. He, secondly, uses these words in connection with mathematical proofs which signal 'new discoveries'. Wittgenstein sees these as extending mathematics and talks of them as 'inventions'.

In both cases logic is concerned with the limits or boundaries of what we regard as permissible and find intelligible. In the latter kind of example a case is made for altering these limits. First let us consider the first kind of case.

When Wittgenstein says here that 'there is no compulsion' he is concerned to combat a common idea about the nature of the kind of necessity or inexorability that belongs to logic and mathematics: 'What if I don't? Suppose I still refuse to accept the conclusion?' 'Then (as Achilles said to the Tortoise) Logic would take you by the throat and *force* you to do so.' For 'Logic' you can read 'the principles of logic' or 'the structure of the propositions in question'. Wittgenstein denies that there is anything of this kind, whether *up* in a heaven, or world of purely intelligible forms (Plato), in the structure of the understanding (Kant), or *within* the impure forms of our propositions (*Tractatus*), to force our hand or our thoughts. But he did not think that we could continue with our use of words any old how, that our words do not commit us in certain ways for the future, that there is no logical necessity in the steps that we take in our deductive reasonings and calculations.

He did not deny this necessity; he was concerned to understand its source, to get clear about what it amounts to. In short, he was not rejecting this notion; he was concerned to analyse it.

So Wittgenstein denied that the meaning or structure of our propositions is the source of the necessity we find in deductive inferences and mathematical calculations, and so rejected the analytic view of necessary truth. If anything he reversed the relation we find in such a view between meaning and necessity. Propositions which we regard as necessary are rules of our language-games; they characterise our language-games. They are formulations of established practices with words, and it is these practices which give meaning to our words. Of course, so far nothing has been said about the sense in characterising these rules as *propositions* and of attributing *truth* to them, or about the source of the necessity we find in them. But Wittgenstein insists that it does not come from anything more fundamental.

'Logical inference (he says) is a transition that is justified if it follows a particular paradigm, and whose rightness is not dependent on anything else.'[11] The paradigm itself is not responsible to anything more fundamental: 'It is akin to what is arbitrary.'[12] But it is involved in the way we do a great many things. This explains, partly, why we treat it as unimpeachable, but it does not justify it. It is, however, also akin to what is non-arbitrary.[13] There is a sense in which one may even ask for its justification.[14]

In a logical inference the premises commit one who accepts them to a particular conclusion, and its justification is the process of bringing this out. But nothing *in this sense* commits one to any rules of grammar or principles of inference. One accepts them in learning to speak, to use words in certain ways. Nor does a language-game commit one to a grammar, since taking part in the language-game *is* speaking in a particular grammar. It isn't as if one who takes part in the language-game is unable to escape certain grammatical requirements. As Wittgenstein puts it: 'Do not say "one cannot", but say instead: "it doesn't exist in this game". Not: "one can't castle in draughts" but – "there is no castling in draughts".'[15] One can follow different rules, only then one would be 'speaking of something else'.[16]

Someone may say: 'The rules of grammar or the propositions which express them are not themselves necessary in the same way that the logical steps we take in deductive arguments are necessary. For they do not have a deductive justification. They determine what steps we take in particular cases but are not themselves determined by more general rules.' This, however, would be to forget that what gives substance or content to any such rule are the logical steps we take in innumerable cases. The inexorability of the rule is thus nothing but the inexorability which these steps have in particular cases for all those who speak the language.

When Wittgenstein compared rules of grammar with the rules of a game he did not mean to deny this inexorability. He said that the rules of chess are arbitrary in a way that rules of grammar are not. He contrasted the rules of chess with the theory of chess (1939). Thus whereas one can modify the game of chess and play in accordance with different rules, one cannot mate one's opponent with two knights alone. This is a necessary truth within the theory of chess, and it takes for granted the rules of chess. It is fixed or determined, and therefore not arbitrary, in the way that each step in the development of a formal series is determined by the rule of progression.[17] But, of course, there is nothing binding about the rules of chess themselves, as there is about principles of inference, mathematical axioms, or other rules of grammar. Wittgenstein does not deny this. On the contrary, he insists on the contrast.[18]

So what makes rules of grammar and the steps we take in accordance with them inexorable for us? What makes the propositions in which they are stated necessary? In what respect are rules of grammar 'akin to what is non-arbitrary'? In what sense are alternative steps ruled out for us? Wittgenstein's discussion of these questions is closely related to his later discussion in *On Certainty* of what makes propositions which belong to 'the scaffolding of our thought' beyond question for us. We regard them as unquestionable, indubitable, unassailable. That we regard *some* things in this way is part of speaking, reasoning, judging. *What* in particular we so regard is part of our natural history. It is both dependent on the kind of beings we are, the kind of environment in which we live, and also makes us the kind of beings we are. We do not *choose* what we are to regard as unassailable: 'Thinking and inferring (like counting) is of course bounded for us, not by an arbitrary definition, but by natural limits corresponding to the body of what can be called the role of thinking and inferring in our life.'[19]

In other words, what we regard as unassailable, what paths we follow in our calculations and deductions, the very character of the language we speak and the mathematics we develop, depend to a large extent on certain natural, matter-of-course reactions which we exhibit in particular situations – reactions that are widely shared among those who speak the same language. There is a two-way dependence between the language we speak and the kind of life we live. This means that what we regard as unquestionable and untouchable will also depend on the various activities that have a prominent place in our life, in the weave of which we use language, and on the interests we develop in the context of these activities. In these respects rules of grammar, principles of logic and mathematical axioms differ from rules of games, and they are akin to what is not arbitrary.

If mathematics did not have an employment 'in civil life' then indeed it would be no more than a game or pastime. In that case the various transitions and transformations within it would not have the force of calculation, mathematical propositions would not express necessary truths for us. It is not logical inference for me to make a change from one formation to another if such formations do not have a linguistic function apart from this transformation.[20] Thus the formations or sentences do not merely occur in formal proofs and systems in which deductions are made from one to the other. They occur in contexts in which they are used to say something, and the deductions are themselves carried out in such contexts. In other words, the concepts that occur in the rules which govern them are used in propositions which are true or false.[21] The rules themselves have a use or linguistic function in 'civil life'.

It is this that enables us to refer to the statement of these rules as *propositions* and to attribute *truth* to them. They are thus at once rules of linguistic practice characterising different language-games and also instruments of language used in various language-games. No more and no less so than propositions which express contingent truths: They are 'a different part of speech'.[22] Their unfalsifiability is a matter of their role in our language and their necessity comes from our having come to depend on this role in so much of our talk and thought. Propositions which express necessary truths for us are grounded in the many activities we carry on in our lives, and also in certain very general facts of nature which influence the form of these activities and the concepts we develop in connection with them. This is one reason why they are unassailable: They are so anchored in all our questions and answers that we cannot touch them.[23]

To be able to imagine any such proposition as false, to contemplate a different possibility, means giving up so much of what we take for granted in our understanding of anything that we find it impossible to do so. No doubt we may succeed in formulating a sentence which would express an alternative to a necessary truth. But we would fail to make any sense of it. As Wittgenstein puts it: We cannot fill it with personal content: we cannot really go along with it – personally, with our intelligence. He compares this with someone's inability to make sense of a particular sequence of notes, to sing it with expression. Such a man may say: 'I cannot respond to it.'[24] This sequence of notes goes against the grain of his whole understanding of music. To be able to sing it with expression he would have to give that up. But this would preclude his singing it, or any other sequence of notes, with expression. It is the same with the logical step I am trying to reverse, the grammatical proposition I am trying to imagine as false. For my intelligence is bound up with my commitment to the norms of intelligibility with which it belongs, and these go through most aspects of my life. When I try to reverse what is in question the whole mechanism of my understanding jams.

A proposition which is necessarily true is thus one which has a special position in our life and language. For different propositions to occupy such a position much in our life and language and, therefore, outlook and understanding would have to be different. Hence given our language, outlook, interests and matter-of-course reactions, and also certain contingent features of the environment in which we live, we cannot countenance abandoning them and letting others occupy their place. It is here that the source of their necessity lies. The word 'must' expresses our inability to depart from a concept-formation.[25] What holds the concept-formation fast for us is its employment in so much of our life and all those achievements in understanding bound up with it.

We see that when Wittgenstein says that 'there is no logical compulsion' he is concerned to combat certain misconceptions about the sense in which the premises we accept commit us to the conclusions that follow from them, and the nature of the truth and necessity of the propositions in which we formulate this commitment. He is *not* claiming that the idea of logical necessity is itself a misconception. In this he differs from Quine.

He is also saying, secondly, that the practices we accept do not commit us to any of the extensions which may be proposed to us, as they are in mathematics by proofs which initiate new concept-formations. The point is that such proofs mimic deductive moves where there are no deductive connections. What is missing here is the agreed reaction, the established practice, to which they attempt to be a precursor. If they succeed in persuading people they *create* a deductive connection. But until then there are no deductive connections, and so no necessary truths.[26] Here the claim that 'there is no logical compulsion' means that we need not go along with such a proof.

To bring together the two connections in which Wittgenstein speaks like this: what there is not in either case is something independent of our practice with the symbols in question, whether outside or within our language, forcing us to conform to it. But what there *is* in the former case and *not* in the latter is an established practice and the connections in our life and culture in which the practice operates. It is this that makes the difference between a necessary truth and the mere proposal of one. So when Wittgenstein says that 'there is no logical compulsion' he is rejecting different things in the two connections in the course of a unitary account. In the first connection it is a confused account of logical necessity that he rejects, in the second he denies that there is any logical necessity before it has been created: 'The proof puts a new paradigm among the paradigms of the language.'[27] But it has to be taken up by us. When that happens we are, as it were, taken over by events.

Does this mean that logical necessity is a fiction which we create? And how far does Wittgenstein's discussion support Quine's thesis? This is the question I wish to consider next.

V. QUINE AND WITTGENSTEIN: A COMPARISON

Quine has the idea, in common with the Positivists and Empiricists whom he criticises, that if there is any logical necessity it must be something which inheres in our symbols and compels us to use them in the ways in which we do – e.g. when we draw valid inferences. He cannot find it there, so he rejects the notion of logical necessity. Because he cannot find an alternative to the analytic account, rejecting that leaves him in a vacuum: 'Any statement can be held true come what may, if we make drastic enough adjustments elsewhere in the system' (p. 43). Contrast with Wittgenstein's conception of 'natural limits corresponding to the body of what can be called the role of thinking and inferring in our life'.

On Quine's view we have a *choice*; we can reconstruct our whole logic, provided we do so bit by bit – like Neurath's captain. While we have to do so bit by bit if we are to keep afloat we can have a vision of what we are fashioning. On Wittgenstein's view this is an impossibility. Our language, given the logic internal to it, determines what we find thinkable. That language, and its logic, can change; they are not immutable. Yet while they cannot change without a change in the speakers, language has a momentum of its own so that what we can contribute to such a change is very limited. We belong to traditions of thought in which our language and its logic are embedded. We do not manipulate the logic of our language. True, mathematicians can extend mathematics at its peripheries, and an Einstein can adopt an alternative geometry as a better mode of representation for his very specialised findings. But extending mathematics is not re-fashioning mathematics, and the suitability of an alternative geometry to the physicist's specialist purposes does not make it a branch of physics. That we can, in this way, choose between alternative calculi does not destroy the character of the calculus chosen as a calculus.

Wittgenstein, like Quine, was critical of the Platonic, realist view of mathematics and logical necessity. He recognised that our laws of inference are not eternal and immutable.[28] But, unlike Quine, he did not embrace a nominalistic view; he did not think that the fact that e.g. our mathematics is not immutable means that the truths of mathematics are not eternal. The timeless character of these truths is a matter of their role in our language. The truths expressed by mathematics may be characterised as 'outside time', as Plato did. But this does not mean that our practice of mathematics is itself outside time, not subject to change. Conversely, the temporal character of the practice does not impugn the timelessness of mathematical truths. As Rhees once put it: 'What we call arithmetic has nothing necessary about it.' But it does not follow from this that the truths of arithmetic are not necessary truths.

There is a sense in which their necessity depends on us and on the kind of life and culture we have developed. 'If you multiply x by y you get z, and anyone who does so *must* get the same result.' Wittgenstein asks what 'must' means here. Having criticised the kind of view Achilles expresses in what he says to the Tortoise, he now says that the MUST above is 'the expression of an attitude towards the technique of calculation, which comes out everywhere in our life. The emphasis of the *must* corresponds only to the inexorableness of this attitude both to the technique of calculating and to a host of related techniques.'[29]

This is by no means a subjectivist or sceptical view of the kind we find in Hume: necessity cannot be found in objects, so it can only be found in the mind. Nor is it its modern counterpart: It cannot be found in objects, empirical or ideal, so it can only be found in language. In fact, Wittgenstein's account stands to this latter view as Kant's account of necessity stands to that of Hume, except for Kant's Platonism. The latter is the analytic view which both Wittgenstein and Quine reject, and which earlier Kant had rejected.

However for Quine the alternatives in question exhaust the possibilities here. It cannot be found in objects; there can be no *de re* necessities. It cannot be found in the structures of the understanding, as Kant had claimed. It cannot be found in language, as Logical Positivists had argued. Therefore, it cannot be found anywhere. So the distinction between necessary and contingent truths is a spurious one.

Not so for Wittgenstein. The fact that no law or rule can be inexorable *in itself* does not mean that it cannot be inexorable *for us* – any more than the fact that the lines on a page are a dead sign ($\rightarrow$) and that the arrow does not point by virtue of what it is itself, independently of those practices with which we surround it, means that it is incapable of pointing, or that its meaning is a psychic thing.[30]

The *attitude* which Wittgenstein speaks of is part of a concept-formation. He would say that the possibility of any concept-formation demands that we should take such an attitude towards certain things, and to certain moves or transitions within a language-game, that we should regard certain propositions in which these moves are generalised as unassailable. But we do not choose what to take this attitude towards, what to regard as unassailable or beyond question. We do not have any reason for regarding as unassailable what we so regard. It is not because doing so gives us the most convenient concept-formation, the one that best satisfies our purposes – as Quine holds.

Quine regards human beings *qua* language users as scientists, as having a single purpose: to understand nature in the way that scientists seek to do. For Wittgenstein, on the other hand, human beings as language users are many-sided, and these many sides develop in a two-way interaction with the language they use. By and large their contribution is not an exercise of their rationality – as it is for Quine.

Wittgenstein asked us to look at language as an instrument. Quine looks on language as an instrument too. But he thinks of men as wielders of this instrument, or instruments, to satisfy their pre-existing purposes. There is no sense in him of the way language moulds men's purposes, of the dependence of men's purposes on the language they speak. When Wittgenstein asked us to look at language as an instrument he wanted us to focus on the work which language does, to consider language in action, and not as dead signs into which their life has to be breathed by some kind of hocus-pocus. When Quine looks at language as an instrument he thinks of it as instrument designed by men for their purposes; he thinks of it as something which men manipulate. There is no sense in Quine of language as having an independent life into which men are born, in which they grow, develop their ability to reason, and find themselves. In this sense language is not man's instrument for understanding nature, in the way that e.g. a microscope or a telescope is, and men's aims are largely those of the language they speak. Men serve the language they speak as much as language serves the men who speak it. Quine's pragmatism is not, as he claims, the result of his abandoning the distinction between necessary and contingent truth; it is one of the sources which led him to its rejection.

Quine is right in thinking that we cannot understand the unassailability of those propositions we characterise as necessary in isolation from propositions which we regard as falsifiable. There is some similarity here between Quine and Wittgenstein. Thus Wittgenstein in *On Certainty*: 'When someone makes a mistake, this can be fitted into what he knows aright' (§74). The point is that otherwise it would not be a mistake, we would not call it a mistake. He gives an example in his *Lectures on Religious Belief*: If someone said, 'Now I'm going to add', and then said: '2 and 21 is 13' etc. I'd say: 'this is no blunder' (p. 62). In other words, for the answer '13' to constitute a mistake, for it to be the wrong answer, incorrect or false, he must mean '2 and 21' as this is normally understood in arithmetic. But if he goes on as Wittgenstein imagines him, we could not say that he is adding numbers in the sense in which we would take him to be adding them for his answer to be mistaken. As Wittgenstein puts it: 'For a blunder, that's too big' (ibid.).

Again: 'All testing, all confirmation and disconfirmation of an hypothesis takes place already within a system . . . The system . . . is the element in which arguments have their life.'[31] The point is the same: The person who is doing the testing would have to agree to a great many things, accept a great many truths. Otherwise what he is doing would not be what we take it to be. When we say, 'He is testing an hypothesis', there is a great deal we take as read. The different things, truths, that he would have to acknowledge as truths for what he is doing to constitute testing an hypothesis belong together, and in that sense form a system.

Once more: 'What reply could I make to adults of a tribe who believe that people sometimes go to the moon . . . and who indeed grant that there are no ordinary means of climbing up to it or flying there? . . . Our whole system of physics forbids us to believe it. For this demands answers to the questions "How did he overcome the force of gravity?", "How could he live without an atmosphere?" and a thousand others which could not be answered.'[32] To-day if we are told that such-and-such an astronaut had been to the moon, we might believe him just because he would answer these questions. That is the credibility of the claim, the possibility of its truth, cannot be separated from credible answers to these many questions. It does not stand alone; we take it to be true if we can also take many other propositions – those that provide answers to these questions – to be true. If someone said 'It is true, whatever the answer to these questions may be', then 'we should feel ourselves intellectually very distant' to him.[33] We couldn't even take it for granted that we understand him, understand what he says, that he means his words as at first he seems to mean them – as in the case of the man who says '2 and 21 is 13'. For what he says to be false, to constitute a blunder, his words must mean what they appear to us to mean. But what he means is not independent of how he answers these questions.

Wittgenstein asks: We say that an empirical proposition can be tested, but how? And he points out that the giving of grounds comes to an end and that what we reach here is not an ungrounded presupposition, but an ungrounded way of acting.[34] And further down he says that the questions that we raise, the ones we seek an answer to if the proposition we are interested in is to be taken as credible 'depend on the fact that some propositions are exempt from doubt, are as it were like hinges on which those (i.e. our questions and doubts) turn'.[35] 'That is to say, it belongs to the *logic* of our scientific investigations that certain things are *in deed* not doubted.'[36]

The similarity between Quine and Wittgenstein here is obvious. However, unlike Quine, Wittgenstein does not think of the propositions to which we take such an attitude as 'postulates' or 'assumptions', as anything we can play around with and readjust in the service of theory-constructions. Thus Quine: 'If this view is right (viz. his view of empirical confirmation) it becomes folly to seek a boundary between . . . statements which hold contingently on experience and . . . statements which hold come what may. Any statement can be held true come what may, if we make drastic enough adjustments elsewhere in the system' (p. 43). Wittgenstein had said: 'If I want the door to turn, the hinges must stay put.'[37] Quine would go along with this, but he would add that we can always adjust our hinges and give our door a new centre around which to turn. But Wittgenstein would say that given such a new centre the door that turns would no longer be the same. A new centre would alter the identity of our questions and so of the answers we were seeking, it would alter the sense we could make of the words which express the propositions whose confirmation we seek. Quine says: 'A conflict with experience at the periphery occasions readjustments in the interior of the field. Truth values have to be redistributed over some of our statements' (p. 42). I am suggesting that you cannot do this without altering the meaning and identity of the statements. Such a redistribution would involve a change in concept-formation. This is precisely the point which Strawson and Grice make in their paper 'In Defence of a Dogma'.

Put the point this way. There is still a distinction between giving up a contingent truth, i.e. when a proposition believed to be true is disconfirmed within a system in the way explained, and giving up a necessary truth. The latter involves accepting a new concept-formation.

Wittgenstein says that propositions which we regard as unassailable, and so as expressing a necessary truth, 'are a different part of speech', they are different instruments of language. We cannot regard them as falsifiable and reject them as false without changing their status or role in language. If we do so, the propositions falsified are no longer *the same* as those that were necessarily true. In short, the rejection of the idea that logic is immutable (the Platonic view) does not entail the rejection of the distinction between necessary and contingent truth.

Quine, in some ways, resembles the philosophical sceptic who having recognised that the norms and criteria we take for granted in our inductive and deductive justifications cannot themselves be justified, claims that those justifications are spurious. For Quine, having recognised that propositions can only be necessary within a system, concludes that since the system itself cannot be necessary, the necessity of any proposition within it cannot be real necessity.

6 Language and Experience

I. QUINE'S CRITIQUE OF EMPIRICISM

Quine's critique of empiricism consists of his critique of what he calls 'the two dogmas of empiricism'. We have considered his critique of 'the first dogma', namely the distinction between necessary and contingent truths, and we found that it is no dogma, i.e. that this distinction is not spurious. Furthermore it is not the exclusive property of empiricism. What is so is the analytic view of necessary truths. For that view implies the rejection of the possibility of *de re* necessities and of any a priori knowledge of nature. Such a possibility is clearly incompatible with empiricism, and empiricism is right to want to reject it. But what it puts in its place is inadequate. So Quine is right to criticise it. However he, in his turn, is wrong to reject the distinction between necessary and contingent truths as spurious.

The second of Quine's 'dogmas of empiricism' is what he calls 'the dogma of reductionism'. This is the view that a proposition, if it is significant, must have a basis in experience from which it can be logically derived. That is the significance of the proposition rests on this relation between the proposition and the experience which would confirm or verify it. Quine rejects this view of a one-to-one relation between a proposition and the experience that would confirm it if true. In its place he puts the 'counter-suggestion . . . that our statements about the external world face the tribunal of sense experience not individually but only as a corporate body' (p. 41). His view is that experience or observation can confirm or disconfirm an individual proposition only given certain assumptions. He expounds his positive account

106

of confirmation in the last section of 'Two Dogmas of Empiricism', in 'Epistemology Naturalised', and in chapter 2 of *The Web of Belief*. In this chapter I shall draw mainly on his statement in 'Epistemology Naturalised'.

An observation does not conflict with a proposition singly but together with other propositions. Quine refers to such propositions together as a system or theory. He says that when an observation shows that a system of beliefs must be overhauled, it leaves us to choose which of those interlocking beliefs to revise.[1] In *The Web of Belief* he talks in terms of beliefs and their revision, and in 'Two Dogmas of Empiricism' he speaks in terms of statements and their re-evaluation – the redistribution of truth-values over some of our statements (p. 42). A proposition may be said to make certain claims or to imply certain consequences which if realised would confirm it:

> The typical statement about bodies has no fund of experiential implications it can call its own. A substantial mass of theory, taken together, will commonly have experiential implications . . . Sometimes . . . an experience implied by a theory fails to come off; and then, ideally, we declare the theory false. But the failure falsifies only a block of theory as a whole, a conjunction of many statements. The failure shows that one or more of these statements is false, but it does not show which.[2]

So what confronts 'the tribunal of sense experience' is not an individual proposition, but a corporate body or system of propositions. Ultimately this body of propositions between which we have to choose when an unwelcome observation rocks the boat is 'the whole of science': 'The unit of empirical significance is the whole of science' (p. 42). We always try to restrict our choice; but the more earth-shaking the unwelcome observation the wider this sphere. Propositions we would not normally contemplate revising are admitted into the melting pot. For instance, the postulate of the conservation of mass is abandoned and replaced by Einstein's postulate of the conversion of mass into energy ($E = mc^2$). Hence Quine makes no distinction between those propositions we are not normally prepared to revise and those that are vulnerable to falsification. For, he argues, the difference between them is only one of degree. In exceptional cases we may have to give up or revise propositions which we have so far regarded as unassailable. So he uses the analogy of a field of force and distinguishes between propositions that lie at its boundaries and those that are at the interior of this field, their distance to the centre being a relative one. Those that are most vulnerable to experience lie at the edges of the field; they are what Quine calls observation statements, those that are least vulnerable lie at the interior; they are 'the logical laws'.

The more remote a proposition from the edge or periphery of the field the less justified we are in attributing a content to it individually (p. 43): 'The typical statement about bodies has no fund of experiential implications it can call its own.'[3] But in the limiting case of observation statements at the edge of the field this is otherwise: 'The observation sentence, situated at the sensory periphery of the body scientific, is the minimal verifiable aggregate; it has an empirical content all its own and wears it on its sleeve.'[4]

If observation statements have an empirical content all their own and typical statements about bodies have no fund of experiential implications they can call their own, it would seem to follow that observation statements cannot be statements about bodies or physical objects. In other words, statements about physical objects cannot qualify as observation statements. In any case, Quine holds physical objects to be 'theoretical posits'. As such, statements about them cannot be at the periphery of 'the body scientific', nor constitute 'the minimal verifiable aggregate'. Quine recognises the problem but rejects the conclusion: 'Observation sentences are commonly about enduring bodies – cats, mats, tables. How is this possible? How can a sentence about bodies be at the same time an observation sentence, for which the whole occasion for affirmation is the observable present?'[5] His answer is that physical object propositions are epistemologically primitive, that we learn them ostensively 'as wholes', and that we could neither formulate nor understand 'physical theory' if we did not already grasp such propositions: 'We get on into theory afterwards, bit by bit, as we learn to dismember the observation sentences and make further use of their component words.'[6]

I agree with Quine about the epistemological, and I would add logical, priority of physical object propositions and about their centrality to our language. But I reject his view of physical objects as 'theoretical posits' or 'constructs'. I also reject his view of language as 'the body scientific'. But I agree that, normally, most of our observations, and certainly those that are relevant to physics, are made at the level of physical object language: we observe butterflies, the colour of litmus paper, the rise of the mercury in the thermometer.

Now Quine's positive account of the confirmation of our beliefs and the propositions in which we express them involves a relativity which, beyond a certain point, he finds unwelcome: 'When an observation shows that a system of beliefs must be overhauled, it leaves us to choose which of those interlocking beliefs to revise.' But if this were always so, how could we ever make an observation? What would we say we had observed on a particular occasion? Would we not have the same choice in saying what it was we had observed – i.e. in identifying and describing it? Quine's notion of an observation sentence is an attempt to escape such a regress.

If he had been willing to admit sense-data statements into his scheme he would not have had this difficulty. But he rejects these: 'No sufficient purpose is served by positing subjective sensory objects.'[7] He gives three reasons: (i) 'We cannot hope to make such objects suffice to the exclusion of physical objects.' 'Immediate experience simply will not, of itself, cohere as an autonomous domain. References to physical things are largely what hold it together.'[8] (ii) 'We do not need sense-data in addition to physical objects, as a means e.g. of reporting illusions and uncertainties.'[9] (iii) 'We also do not need sensory objects to account for our knowledge or discourse of physical objects themselves.'[10] Instead Quine prefers to talk, barbarically, of 'physical irritations of the subject's surfaces'.[11] His defence is that while sense-data are subjective the 'stimulation of sense receptors' is something objective.

In 'Epistemology Naturalised' Quine refers to the Logical Positivists, and in particular to Carnap, who thought of the language of sense-data as epistemologically prior and tried to reconstruct our knowledge of the world by searching for deductive links between the propositions in which it is expressed and propositions about sense-data thought to provide their ultimate evidence. These philosophers failed, Quine claims, because the propositions in which our knowledge is expressed 'largely do not have their private bundles of empirical consequences'.[12] This is the point that they do not confront the tribunal of sense experience singly or individually. So the problem which they were trying to solve has to be tackled differently. This problem is 'to see how evidence relates to theory, and in what ways one's theory of nature transcends any available evidence'.[13] But how does sensory evidence lead us to make the statements that we do make? In his more recent writings Quine answers this question in terms of a language that applies to computers: 'The human subject is accorded a certain experimentally controlled input – certain patterns of irradiation in assorted frequencies, for instance – and in the fullness of time the subject delivers as output a description of the three-dimensional external world and its history.'[14] This then is what observation sentences record: the input, the patterns of sensory stimulation of an organism with a history of various other such stimulations. We shall see that this is hardly an advance on sense-data language.

Quine would not agree. He thinks that reference to stimulation resolves the 'stubborn old enigma of epistemological priority': 'In the old epistemological context the conscious form had priority, for we were out to justify our knowledge of the external world by rational reconstruction, and that demands awareness. Awareness ceased to be demanded when we gave up trying to justify our knowledge of the external world by rational reconstruction. What to count as observation now can be settled in terms of the stimulation of sensory receptors, let consciousness fall where it may.'[15] But this excursion into biology or psychology (call it what you will) is very much in conflict with the rational pragmatism of Quine.

So observation is equated with the stimulation of sensory receptors: 'It is simply the stimulations of our sensory receptors that are best looked upon as the input to our cognitive mechanism.'[16] As for the question of epistemological priority, Quine answers it as follows: 'A is epistemologically prior to B if A is causally nearer than B to the sensory receptors.'[17] What does he mean? This is what I understand. Supposing I am concerned to know whether p is true. I put myself in a position where I use my senses. The more I use and have to rely on what I already accept as true the less does my verdict depend on 'the deliverances of my senses' at the time. So the sentence which expresses proposition p would not be in close or direct causal proximity to the sensory receptors. My verdict, True or False, is not very strongly conditioned by the present sensory stimulation that I receive. It follows that the sentence in question is not an observation sentence. For a sentence is an observation sentence 'if our verdict depends only on the sensory stimulation present at the time'.[18]

But how can it depend solely on that? To assess the truth of an observation report we must understand the language in which it is expressed. That brings in knowledge we acquired in the past in learning the language. Quine refers to this as 'stored information'. We must, therefore, he says, revise our criterion, relax our definition: 'A sentence is an observation sentence if all verdicts on it depend on present sensory stimulation and on no stored information beyond what goes into understanding the sentence.'[19] But how are we to distinguish between stored information that is relevant solely to our understanding of the sentence and stored information that goes beyond that?

Quine points out that 'this is the problem of distinguishing between analytic truth, which issues from the mere meanings of words, and synthetic truth, which depends on more than meanings'. He adds: 'I have long maintained that this distinction is illusory.'[20] He says that we can round this problem by supposing that all fluent speakers of the language would bring the same stored information relevant to the understanding of sentences. In respect of *other* stored information they would diverge. This would make their verdicts on the truth of propositions expressed in the language they share differ, save in the case of observation sentences. For these are defined as those sentences to the verdict on which such information is irrelevant. So Quine concludes: 'An observation sentence is one on which all speakers of the language give the same verdict when given the same concurrent stimulation.' It is one 'that is not sensitive to differences in past experiences within the speech community'.[21]

Quine then considers the kind of question that was raised by Professor Hanson in the first chapter, 'Observation', of his book *Patterns of Discovery*: Does not what anyone *sees* depend on the language they speak, the theories they understand and the culture to which they belong? If it does, can there be a pure sense of 'seeing', one that is solely dependent on sensory stimulation? Not surprisingly Quine's discussion of this question is utterly inadequate.

It is obvious that Quine who has flirted with relativism so freely wants to escape it with observation sentences. He cannot let relativism touch them, and he thinks he can avoid it by reducing observation to sensory stimulation. He says that doing so 'accords perfectly with the traditional role of the observation sentence as the court of appeal of scientific theories'.[22] So, despite all his sophisticated detour, Quine is back where he left his brother positivists behind: (i) 'Observation sentences are the repository of evidence for scientific hypotheses.'[23] (ii) 'They afford the only entry to a language.' My claim is that Quine is the old positivist sheep in wolves' clothing. As he himself puts it: 'It is no shock to the preconceptions of old Vienna to say that epistemology now becomes semantics. For epistemology remains centred as always on evidence, and meaning remains centred as always on verification; and evidence is verification.'[24] He goes on: What is likelier to shock preconceptions is that meaning, once we get beyond observation sentences, ceases in general to have any clear applicability to single sentences.' This is Quine's view that 'the unit of empirical significance is the whole of science'. Secondly, what is likelier to shock preconceptions is 'that epistemology merges with psychology, as well as with linguistics'.[25] This is the view that the study of the way evidence relates to theory and the way theory goes beyond evidence is the study of the way 'experimentally controlled input . . . in the fullness of time' issues in an output of 'descriptions of the three-dimensional external world and its history'.

II.   QUINE'S BRAND OF EMPIRICISM AND ITS CRITIQUE

For all his critique of empiricism Quine is himself an empiricist and he makes no secret of it. But his empiricism shares with the empiricism and positivism he has criticised what I regard as the real dogmas of empiricism – that our language is ultimately based on sense experience and that all our knowledge arises out of this experience: that the senses are the source of all our knowledge and all our concepts. The dictum is that 'there is nothing in the intellect, and so in science, that was not previously in the senses'.

What is in the senses, whether one views this as 'raw experience' or 'patterns of stimulation', is thought of as something that precedes language and explains it – given our physical make up.

In his earlier essay 'Two Dogmas of Empiricism' (1951) we have such a notion of *experience*. In his later work *Word and Object* (1960) and 'Epistemology Naturalised' (1961) it gives way to the notion of *the stimulation of sense receptors* – thought of as having greater objectivity. So, on the one hand, we have 'the flux of experience', 'patterns of stimulation', and, on the other hand, we have the particular language or conceptual scheme we have developed. The latter represents our way of organising this flux of experience or stimulation – *language as an instrument*. But however experience is organised or 'conceptualised' the possibility of the truth of the sentences of the organising language *ultimately* rests on the relation between these sentences and the unorganised, raw experience – *meaning and verification*. Quine's empiricism combines this kind of pragmatism with a modified form of verificationism.

He writes: 'Physical objects are postulated entities which round out and simplify our account of the flux of experience, just as the introduction of irrational numbers simplifies the laws of arithmetic . . . From a phenomenalistic point of view, the conceptual scheme of physical objects is a convenient myth, simpler than the literal truth and yet containing that literal truth as a scattered part' (p. 18). Quine, we saw, rejects the 'phenomenalistic point of view', the attempt to describe facts in terms of sense-data. But what facts? Does he not agree that they cannot be identified independently of a language or conceptual scheme? He is ambivalent on this point.

On the negative side we have his 'ontological relativism': What counts as fact for us is relative to our conceptual scheme. Different conceptual schemes are not commensurable in the sense that their respective sentences are not intertranslatable. But though not intertranslatable, they are 'interpretable' or 're-interpretable' in one another. Quine discusses this question at length in his essay 'Ontological Relativity'. There he takes the view that there is nothing independent of different conceptual schemes, no common measure, against which they can be measured. But they can still be compared (so Quine argues) by measuring them against each other.

He says: 'A question of the form "What is an F?" can be answered only by recourse to a further term: "An F is a G." The answer makes only relative sense: sense relative to the uncritical acceptance of "G".'[26] 'When we ask, "Does 'rabbit' refer to rabbits?" someone can counter with the question: "Refer to rabbits in what sense of 'rabbits'?" thus lamenting a regress; and we need the background language [he calls it 'home theory' further down] to regress into. The background language gives the query sense, if only relative sense – sense relative in turn to this background language. Querying reference in any more absolute way would be like asking absolute position, or absolute velocity, rather than position or velocity relative to a given frame of reference. Also it is very much like asking whether our neighbour may not systematically see everything upside down, or in complementary colour, forever undetectably.'[27] He goes on to argue, I think quite rightly, that this regress is not infinite or vicious: 'In practice of course we end the regress of co-ordinate systems by something like pointing. And in practice we end the regress of background languages, in discussions of reference, by acquiescing in our mother tongue and taking its words at face value.'[28]

Quine can reject the 'phenomenalistic point of view' without going back on his relativism. What is more, I believe that, purged of his 'ontologism', that position is defensible. In the passage I quoted earlier Quine says that the concept of physical object 'simplifies our account of the flux of experience'. 'Our account of the flux of experience' – this is short for 'the statements we would have to make in a phenomenalistic language in an attempt to say what is true'. 'True about what?' Answer: 'True about the things we are interested to talk about.' So far so good. 'Flux of experience' may have been used here as simply an expression that belongs to phenomenalistic language, just as 'physical object' is an expression that belongs to physical object language.

But are the facts stated in phenomenalistic language, when the statements made in it are true, *the same set of facts* as those stated in physical object language, when statements made in it are true? I said that Quine is ambivalent in his answer to this question, just as he is ambivalent over the question of the epistemological priority of phenomenalistic language. In other words, while he recognises that the expression 'experience' or 'the flux of experience', if it has any sense at all, must have sense *within* a language, he nevertheless gives it a commanding position outside any language: 'Two cardinal tenets of empiricism remained

unassailable, . . . and so remain to this day. One is that whatever
evidence there *is* for science *is* sensory evidence. The other . . . is
that all inculcation of meanings of words must rest ultimately on
sensory evidence. Hence the continuing attractiveness of the idea
of a logical reconstruction in which the sensory content of
discourse would stand forth explicitly.'[29]

Quine's empiricist theories of knowledge and meaning, we
have seen, converge through their connection with observation
sentences: (i) 'Natural knowledge is to be based somehow on
sense experience.'[30] 'The observation sentence is the court of
appeal of scientific theories.'[31] This on the side of knowledge. (ii)
'The sort of meaning that is basic to translation, and to the
learning of one's own language, is necessarily empirical meaning
and nothing more. A child learns his first words and sentences by
hearing and using them in the presence of appropriate stimuli.'[32]
'The observation sentence is the corner stone of semantics. For it
is . . . fundamental to the learning of meaning.'[33] This on the side
of meaning. What, on Quine's view, the 'inculcation of meanings
of words' and the verification of theories and other statements
ultimately rest on is the stimulation of sensory receptors: 'What to
count as observation now can be settled in terms of the
stimulation of sensory receptors, let consciousness fall where it
may . . . It is simply the stimulations of our sensory receptors that
are best looked upon as the input of our cognitive mechanism.'[34]
'The stimulation of his sensory receptors is all the evidence
anybody has had to go on, ultimately, in arriving at his picture of
the world.'[35]

I shall put beside these one last passage from Quine's older
essay, 'Two Dogmas of Empiricism', to illustrate the kind of
priority he gives to the notion of evidence – conceived in his later
essays as the stimulation of sensory receptors: 'As an empiricist I
continue to think of the conceptual scheme of science as a tool,
ultimately, for predicting future experience in the light of past
experience. Physical objects are conceptually imported into the
situation as convenient intermediaries . . ., as irreducible posits
comparable, epistemologically, to the gods of Homer . . . The
myth of physical objects is epistemologically superior . . . in that
it has proved more efficacious . . . as a device for working a
manageable structure into the flux of experience' (p. 44). 'They
expedite [with greater efficacy] our dealings with sense
experience' (p. 45).

The idea here seems to be that whatever conceptual scheme we adopt we have one and one aim only: to deal with, organise, or expedite in the most efficacious manner 'the flux of experience'. This is on the other side of the question I raised above and claimed Quine to be ambivalent about – the question whether we can intelligibly speak of foundations common to our divergent conceptual schemes, common because identifiable independently of these schemes for all of which they constitute foundations. This, I believe, is the real dogma of empiricism. In the above passage 'flux of experience' is *not* used simply as an expression that belongs to phenomenalistic language – as 'physical object' is one that belongs to physical object language. It is intended to refer to something that has absolute existence.

Combining this absolutist view with his relativism we can attribute to Quine the view that there is nothing independent of different conceptual schemes, with their relative ontologies, save the flux of experience or the barrage of stimulation to which our sensory receptors are continually subjected. It is *this* that is differently worked out and packaged into very different products by different conceptual schemes. However these two views are incompatible.

Contrast once more with Wittgenstein. (i) Quine: 'The myth of physical objects [or 'the concept of physical object'] is a device for working a manageable structure into the flux of experience.' Wittgenstein: 'Concepts help us to comprehend things. They correspond to a particular way of dealing with situations.'[36] There is no mention of experience here. The words 'things' and 'situations' which Wittgenstein uses are meant to refer in a general way to what we face in our lives *as language users* – that is as human beings already endowed with language, and *not* as biological organisms endowed with sensory receptors. (ii) Quine: 'The stimulation of his sensory receptors is all the evidence anybody has had to go on, ultimately, in arriving at his picture of the world.' Wittgenstein: 'I did not get my picture of the world by satisfying myself of its correctness; nor do I have it because I am satisfied of its correctness. No: it is the inherited background against which I distinguish between true and false.'[37] Here contrast Quine's account of the way we acquire language with Wittgenstein's account of the kind of training and instruction through which we learn to speak and acquire beliefs.

To take up the first point of contrast first. Wittgenstein would have said that the confrontation and comparison of a proposition with what makes it true or false takes place within a particular grammar. This is very different from Quine's claim that experience can confirm or disconfirm an individual statement only given certain assumptions about the truth and falsity of other statements. To begin with, for Quine, all propositions, except perhaps observation statements, are *hypotheses*, and they all lie on the same continuum or logical space. The idea of 'different grammars', 'different forms of comparison with what would make them true or false' is alien to Quine's conception. What differentiates between the different propositions of this *one* system is the degree of their answerability to experience. Those that are most answerable are the observation statements and those that are least answerable are the propositions of logic and mathematics. Even religious statements, like 'Whatever God wills happens', are treated as hypotheses and, therefore, as belonging to this same 'scientific continuum'. Religious statements, philosophical statements, logical and mathematical propositions keep company with scientific propositions. In this Quine is at one with the Logical Positivists. What differentiates him from them is (i) his refusal to distinguish logical and philosophical propositions from the rest, and (ii) his new theory of confirmation or verification. What aligns him with the Logical Positivists is his treatment of all significant propositions as hypotheses that are logically related (though not in the same way as Logical Positivists had claimed) to observation statements. Wittgenstein's idea of language being made up of different language-games embedded in a culture with various distinctive features is completely alien to Quine's thinking.

I spoke of the confrontation of a proposition with what makes it true or false advisedly, and not, as Quine speaks, of its confrontation with experience. What makes a proposition true or false: this cannot be described without repeating the proposition or some other proposition in the same language. That is what makes a proposition true or false lies in the same grammar as the proposition, and the proposition confronts it within that grammar. Much of what we experience or observe is mediated by the language we speak. We cannot analyse this into or hope to understand it in terms of the stimulation of our sense receptors. Kant had recognised this long ago in his critique of empiricism.

He writes in a letter to Herz: If I had the mentality of a subhuman animal, I might have intuitions (i.e. sensations) but 'I should not be able to know that I have them, and they would therefore be for me, as a cognitive being, absolutely nothing. They might still exist in me . . . as representations . . . exercising influence upon feeling and desire, . . . without my thereby acquiring the least cognition of anything, not even of these my own states.'[38] There are similar passages in his *Critique of Pure Reason*.

Quine tells us to let consciousness drop – 'fall where it may'. Presumably he wishes us to consider the behaviour of the organism. But we cannot do so apart from the circumstances that surround the behaviour. In the case of human beings these are the circumstances of the kind of life that has developed with language. Quine would not deny this. But in what he writes he shows little awareness of the difference this makes to what a human being is capable of experiencing and observing. The notion of stimulation, which is presumably sense experience shorn of all consciousness, cannot bring any of this into focus. That notion belongs with the treatment of human beings as computers.

As for what Quine calls 'empirical meaning', it is not clear to me what he wishes to contrast this with: Empirical meaning as opposed to what sort of meaning? Perhaps he wishes to say that all terms or concepts are empirical terms or concepts, that there are no a priori concepts. This would be parallel to his claim that all sentences express contingent truths or falsehoods, that there are no necessary truths or a priori propositions. He says: 'The sort of meaning that is basic to translation, and to the learning of one's own language, is necessarily empirical meaning and nothing more. A child learns his first words and sentences by hearing and using them in the presence of appropriate stimuli . . . Language is socially inculcated and controlled: the inculcation and control turn strictly on the keying of sentences to shared stimulation. Internal factors may vary *ad libitum* without prejudice to communication as long as the keying of language to external stimuli is undisturbed. Surely one has no choice but to be an empiricist so far as one's theory of linguistic meaning is concerned.'[39] Quine has obviously a very crude conception of what he calls 'internal factors'.[40] But this is a minor point for our present purposes. For the main trouble lies in the crudity of his conception of 'external factors'. He thinks in terms of the organism's reactions to stimuli that impinge on his sense receptors. Whereas what is important are the modes of acting which the child learns as he learns to speak, learning the two in harness. He is not responding to stimuli, but to situations the significance of which cannot be separated from the modes of activity in the weave of which he learns to act.

Wittgenstein speaks of primitive, matter-of-course reactions in which those who speak the same language agree and he emphasises the importance of this kind of agreement for the possibility of language and the learning of it. Such reactions are not based on anything and are constitutive of the basic features and formal concepts of the language we speak. Wittgenstein speaks of them as 'special chapters of human behaviour', as 'prototypes of ways of thinking' of which our language-games are extensions. My relation to what I react to in these ways is part of the concept I have of it. Our concepts, what view we take of things, belong to our ways of acting. What is *ultimate* are the ways of acting we learn and our matter-of-course reactions – those that are primitive as well as those that are learned in the course of acquiring speech. These determine the way external things affect us.

This is very different from, if not diametrically opposed to, Quine's conception of the social control of language turning strictly on the keying of sentences to shared stimulation. I am contrasting Quine's notion of 'shared stimulation', which is indeed fundamental to his empiricism, with Wittgenstein's notion of 'agreement in reactions' which constitutes what he calls 'the limits of empiricism'. Why limits of empiricism? Because, on Wittgenstein's view, our language is not founded on an empirical reality with which we are in contact through sense perception. Rather our language determines the kind of contact we can have with such a reality and our conception of it. And I make no distinction between the form of that reality and our conception of it. As for the kind of language we develop, it is determined, among other things, by the kind of beings we are – the way we find it natural to react to certain situations given a certain kind of training. We could say, in fact, that it is not what we experience that determines the kind of language we speak: but rather the kind of language we have developed determines the kind of experiences we have.

Of course our sense organs are stimulated independently of language. And such stimulation exists independently of language in the sense that we can speak about it and make true and false statements about it – just as we can make true and false statements about tables and chairs. But experience is another matter. It is not the 'inner' aspect of stimulation which Quine has allowed to drop away in his later writings. Of course experience is not confined to creatures who have and speak a language, though it cannot be divorced from action, i.e. it cannot be understood in separation from modes of acting. Most of these modes of acting, in the case of human beings, is bound up with language. And here the kinds of experience we are capable of belong with the language we speak. For this reason experience cannot be made to give foundation to our language. When Wittgenstein describes the acquisition of language he speaks of *training*. What we learn is to act in certain ways, including the use of words. Learning to identify and name things comes later and presupposes that we have already come a certain way.

'The senses provide us with the evidence of the various things we wish to say or claim.' Yes, but this presupposes a language and established methods of comparison. Indeed, science takes its start from the reality of everyday language and the questions asked in it, and it takes for granted many common sense truisms, truths that we accept prior to any scientific investigation – such as that water boils when heated and does not freeze. This is very different from the empiricist claim that 'there is nothing in science, or more generally in the intellect, in thought, which was not first in the senses'. For much of what is first in the senses presupposes those categories of everyday language on which sophisticated scientific language is founded. But the reality of everyday language from which science takes its start is not something that is founded on the senses.

The senses enter the foundations of human knowledge in general and of scientific knowledge in particular in a different way, namely through their peculiar role in the life of those who speak our language. Both *the use of the senses* and *the use of language* are part of our natural history. They are intertwined in the sense that the *ways* in which we use our senses and the activities in which the senses play an important role, such as in scientific observation, are inconceivable apart from the language we speak. Equally, the language we speak is one that has developed in the context of activities in all of which the use of the senses plays an important role.

Put it another way. Seeing, or more generally perceiving, is not something which can be said to give foundation to thinking, since seeing involves thinking or thought. In Kant's language: 'Thoughts without content are empty, intuitions without concepts are blind.'[41]

It seems to me that the main weakness of all forms of empiricism, including the empiricism of Quine, lies in the epistemological priority they accord to the senses. This is done by Quine through the notion of observation sentences in the way we have seen. In place of the epistemological priority of the senses I should like to speak of the interdependence between the use of the senses and the use of language in human life. Notice that I am not speaking of the senses, but of 'the use of the senses'. This is something that we learn, even if such learning presupposes certain unthinking reactions to sensible objects and situations. If we can say that we use the senses within various frameworks, then it should be clear that the frameworks cannot themselves be said to be determined by the senses. As Wittgenstein puts it: 'Do not believe that you have the concept of colour within you because you look at a coloured object – however you look.'[42] In other words, the fact that a creature can see coloured objects does not mean that he knows what a colour is, that he has any concept of colour, with all that this involves. In learning the meanings of words from ostentive definitions we are pointed out things we can see, hear, etc. But we cannot in this way acquire all the concepts that enter our judgements. For to understand an ostensive definition we must already be master of a language.[43]

This does not mean that we have here at play a form of knowledge that goes beyond the senses. No. The empiricist is right in wanting to claim that the senses are all that we have to go by. But he is wrong in the way he pictures us as passive recipients in our capacity to acquire knowledge. Quine does not do so; but he still thinks of the senses too much as 'sense receptors' exposed to certain stimuli. And he does not show sufficient recognition of the background against or the context in which we use our senses when we make observations. His theory of the way propositions confront sense experience as part of a system does not bring this background into focus.

III.   A PERSONAL VERDICT

Quine has been acclaimed as an innovator in philosophy, as someone who has challenged orthodoxies. We have seen what *some* of these challenges amount to.

I think, myself, that he certainly has dexterity and intelligence, but he appeals to what is most brash in us.

He develops what he calls an 'empiricism without dogmas', and he goes beyond that in his later writings. He is drawn towards Nominalism, Behaviourism, Physicalism, Pragmatism, and Verificationism. He tends to look at human beings as computers and at the acquisition of language as a form of programming. He treats language as one big theory in the service of science, and he thinks of philosophy as a branch of science. For all his 'modernism' in the worst sense he is at heart 'old fashioned' in the worst sense. For all his rejection of 'dogmas', he is tied to the apron-strings of Logical Positivism. The logical positivists, with all their crudity, were at least innovators. Quine, on the other hand, for all his innovations, is a backwoodsman. For all his appeal to our age, I do not think that he has emerged from the woods. He does not represent a new dawn in philosophy, but a temporary eclipse.

Summary of the Book

The discussion of this book falls into three parts as its title indicates.

In the first part (chapters 1–4) my main concern is to show that Quine's concept of ontology is untenable. I begin by giving a brief exposition of it (chapter 1). I then argue against Quine's conception of philosophy as concerned with general theoretical issues on a logical par with those that concern the sciences. I take as an example the question of 'the existence of physical objects' and argue that what is at issue here has little to do with existence.

It is important to distinguish between our concept of physical object, which is no ordinary concept, and the philosophical idea of a substratum of the sensible properties of things – *vide* Locke. The former has often been rejected by philosophers as a fiction because they identified it with the latter. I argue that a philosophical discussion that advances our understanding of what is at issue here ought to do two things: (i) It ought to disentangle the two ideas and shed light on what lies at the source of their confusion. (ii) It ought to bring out the way our concept of physical object differs from our concepts of particular things, such as tables, and chairs, and rabbits, and the sense in which it is not open to rejection (chapter 2).

I next consider Quine's conception of language as carrying existential implications to which its speakers are commited (chapter 3). Are there certain beliefs that people assent to as part of speaking a particular language, beliefs which they are not at liberty to question while they speak that language? I consider Wittgenstein's discussion of this question in *On Certainty* and contrast it with Quine's view of the existential commitments of a language. I then criticise Quine's pragmatic conception of language and contrast it with what Wittgenstein was getting at

123

when he stressed the work which language does – a question to which I return later – in chapter 5.

I consider the question 'Are there universals?' as an example of the kind of question Quine characterises as ontological (chapter 4). Once more I distinguish between our concept of the generality inherent in the meanings of words, particularly those of common nouns, and the philosophical idea of the *essence* of a kind, or our *abstract idea* of it, which our general nouns for them are supposed to signify – *vide* Plato and Locke. I consider what the rejection of the latter idea amounts to and argue that it does not commit one to any form of nominalism – any more than does the rejection of the idea of a physical substratum commit one to phenomenalism. But, in any case, neither nominalism nor phenomenalism are theoretical positions, such as that of Lavoisier who rejected Priestley's idea of phlogiston, and neither carry any existential implications. I argue that both nominalism and realism, its philosophical rival, are neutral with regard to the language we speak – a claim which is explicitly contradicted by Quine.

I examine Wittgenstein's rejection of the idea of Platonic essences as well as that of universals as resemblances, both forms of realism, and argue that Wittgenstein's anti-realism is not a form of nominalism. The nominalist confuses the platitudinous claim that things which are called by the same name must have something in common, namely being of the same kind, with the metaphysical claim that they must have something in common over and above this, a common essence which explains why we group them together and call them by the same name.

Quine confuses these two claims. On the one hand, he holds that 'There are attributes' follows immediately from such 'casual statements of commonplace facts' as 'There are red houses, red roses, red sunsets'. On the other hand, he also says that 'there is not in addition to red things an entity named by redness'. Consequently, he thinks that our everyday language or conceptual scheme needs revision. But the platitude that 'There are attributes', like 'There are physical objects', is no ordinary platitude. It is certainly distinct from the metaphysical idea of 'universals as ingredients'. It is the latter that Quine wishes to reject. But that is not something to which our language commits us. Therefore to reject it one does not have to revise the language we speak.

I then turn to Quine's discussion of the question whether there are necessary truths, although he does not himself express it in these terms (chapter 5). He formulates it in terms of the analytic/synthetic distinction and argues that there is no 'fundamental cleavage between truths which are analytic . . . and truths which are synthetic'. This makes for confusion since one can reject the philosophical view that necessary truths are analytic without thereby accepting Quine's conclusion. In fact I would say that the necessary/contingent distinction is a *logical* distinction, whereas the analytic/synthetic distinction is a *philosophical* one. I mean that the former, if it is a genuine distinction, is one that can be seen in our actual use of language. Whereas the latter is a distinction made by philosophers with a view to understanding the nature of the logical distinction, taken as unquestioned.

Quine questions it, however, as well as the empiricist view that it rests on or coincides with the analytic/synthetic distinction. But we must not let Quine's procedure obscure that there are two different things he is questioning here, not one. Secondly, the conclusion he reaches in questioning the notion of analyticity does not support his rejection of the empiricist view that necessary truths are analytic. I would go along with Quine in rejecting that view, but not for the reason that Quine gives, namely that the notion of analyticity cannot be defined without circularity. No doubt it cannot be so defined; but I do not find that a damaging discovery.

I refer to Quine's view that necessary truths are not analytic as his negative thesis, and I take no interest in the formalistic procedure he uses in an attempt to establish it. But I am interested in Quine's discussion of logical necessity and in his positive, albeit sceptical, thesis that there are no propositions which are absolutely unfalsifiable and, therefore, necessary. I argue that, as in other forms of philosophical scepticism, in Quine's positive thesis truth and falsehood are intermingled and so need to be disentangled. I refer to it as his positive thesis because of the positive claim it makes about propositions which we regard as necessarily true.

What it says about these is closely connected with Quine's theory of the confirmation of propositions which we regard as falsifiable. Indeed, they are the two sides of the same coin. Quine holds that these propositions are falsified by experience only because we refuse to give up some *other* propositions which we regard as true. Those that we are unwilling to give up under forseeable circumstances are those that we regard as necessarily true. But there is *no necessity* for us to regard *those* propositions in this way, *no necessity* for us to continue to regard the same propositions in this way. From this Quine draws the conclusion that no proposition is *logically necessary*. This conclusion is distinct from Quine's negative thesis that propositions which we regard as expressing necessary truths are not analytic.

'There is no necessity for us . . . Therefore no proposition is logically necessary.' This argument runs together two different senses of necessity which Wittgenstein tries to sift out when he says: 'There is no logical compulsion.' But again the confusion at work in Quine's sceptical argument can be expressed as follows: What Quine wishes to reject is a defective account of logical necessity, not logical necessity itself. But because he identifies the latter with the former, he cannot reject the account without rejecting that of which it is an account. Indeed, there is a close affinity between this idea of logical necessity as a form of compulsion and the idea of universals as ingredients in the things named which constitute the essence of the kind of thing they are. In the former case we think of the meanings of words and the rules of inference as tracks that keep us on the right course in our inferences; in the latter we think of the meanings of general nouns as blue-prints (*vide* Locke's abstract idea) that keep us on the right course in the classifications of things and in our application of their names. Philosophy here is concerned with misunderstandings concerning the sense in which logic determines the steps in our reasonings and our observations determine our classifications.

What saves Quine from conventionalism in the one case and from nominalism in the other is his pragmatism. I argue that while there is much that is of interest in what Quine puts in place of what he rejects in his discussion of logical necessity it is marred by his pragmatism. I try to bring this out in my comparison of Quine and Wittgenstein.

In the last chapter I am concerned with Quine's empiricism. I consider his account of 'observation sentences' and his notion of 'experience' which, in his later writings, give way to the notion of 'sensory stimulation'. I argue that what he wishes to establish in terms of these notions is incompatible with his relativism. Despite his criticism of what he calls 'the dogma of reductionism' his theory of confirmation according to which our statements confront experience as a system does not really take him outside the orbit of logical positivism. What Quine does not recognise is the way what we are capable of observing and the form of our experiences are determined by the kind of life we live and the language we speak. Of course the subject's past experiences make a difference to his present experiences, and Quine certainly allows for what the subject learns, through being exposed to various stimulations, affecting his delivery of output in the fullness of time. But this is not enough. He argues that what ultimately determines the kind of language we speak, apart from pragmatic considerations, conceived from a narrowly scientific point of view, is experience, conceived in an absolute sense. This is the notion of experience which I criticise and reject. I conclude with some general remarks about the way in which the senses enter the foundations of human knowledge in general and of scientific knowledge in particular.

Notes

All page numbers, where not otherwise specified, refer to Quine's *From a Logical Point of View* (1963). These follow quotations in the text and do not occur in these Notes.

CHAPTER 1 QUINE'S CONCEPTION OF ONTOLOGY

1. It is a 'philosophical' word, one coined by philosophers. While this does not automatically make it an incoherent notion, it does not guarantee its coherence or intelligibility either. Many philosophical notions are little more than symptoms of confusion, however important the difficulties which give rise to such confusions. I shall argue that the notion of ontology is such a notion.
2. Toulmin (1955), p. 128.
3. Berkeley (1950), §51.
4. Quine (1969), p. 99.
5. ibid., p. 103.
6. Berkeley op. cit., §35.
7. ibid., §37.
8. Quine (1969), p. 94.
9. ibid., pp. 48-9.
10. Quine (1975), p. 3.
11. ibid.
12. ibid., p. 234.
13. Compare with Russell in *The Problems of Philosophy*: What the idealist or phenomenalist puts forward is 'a less simple hypothesis, viewed as a means of accounting for the facts of our own life, than the common sense hypothesis that there really are objects independent of us' (p. 10).
14. Quine (1975), pp. 275-6.
15. For a very good discussion of this question see Toulmin and Goodfield, *The Architecture of Matter*, chapter 10, pp. 222-8.
16. See Wittgenstein (1961), 6.341-6.3431.
17. Wittgenstein (1956), Part V, §46.

CHAPTER 2 ONTOLOGY, LANGUAGE AND EXISTENCE

1. Wittgenstein (1963), §194.
2. Ryle (1950), p. 75.

3. In fact I find Ryle's portrait of the peasants in his story as incredible as I find Quine's portrait of Plato shallow. If philosophers can be like savages, this is one respect in which they are sometimes so. Thus Wittgenstein said of Frazer, the anthropologist, that he is 'much more savage than most of his savages'. See 'Remarks on Frazer's "Golden Bough" ', *The Human World*, No. 3, May 1971, p. 34.
4. Ryle (1966), p. 8.
5. Moore (1963), p. 41.
6. ibid., p. 198.
7. Wisdom (1953), p. 145.
8. ibid.
9. ibid., p. 242.
10. Berkeley op. cit. §35.
11. Quine (1969), p. 98.
12. ibid.
13. See Quine (1975), p. 241.
14. ibid., p. 243.
15. Wisdom (1953), p. 137. For a fuller discussion see Dilman (1975), Part I, chapter 7.
16. For a fuller discussion of this question see Dilman (1975), Part I, chapter 3.
17. See ibid., Part I, chapter 2.
18. Wittgenstein (1974a), p. 321.
19. See Wittgenstein (1969b), §35–6, 476–7.
20. I discuss this question in Dilman (1974).
21. See Toulmin and Goodfield (1962), pp. 263–8.

CHAPTER 3   LANGUAGE, THEORY AND BELIEF

1. I shall return to this question in chapter 5, section IV.
2. Wittgenstein (1969b), §143.
3. See ibid., §314–16.
4. ibid., §159.
5. ibid., §160.
6. ibid., §161.
7. ibid., §162.
8. ibid., §170.
9. Wittgenstein (1963), §87.
10. Wittgenstein (1956), Part II, §79.
11. ibid., Part II, §83.
12. See ibid., Part I, §4.
13. See Quine (1963), p. 44.
14. Wittgenstein (1956), Part I, §155.
15. ibid., Part II, §75.
16. ibid., Part V, §2.
17. ibid., Part I, §4. Also see §118.
18. ibid.
19. ibid., Part V, §45.

20. ibid., Part V, §23.
21. ibid., §9.
22. ibid.
23. See my comments in Dilman (1973), Part II.

CHAPTER 4 ARE THERE UNIVERSALS?

1. See Dilman (1981), chapter 2.
2. I have discussed the nature of Moore's 'proof' in Dilman (1975), Part I.
3. See H. H. Price (1953), p. 11.
4. See Wittgenstein (1969a), p. 17.
5. See Dilman (1978).
6. I am indebted to Wisdom who used to put it like this in lectures I attended at Cambridge long ago as an undergraduate.
7. Locke (1959), p. 226.
8. ibid., p. 231.
9. ibid., p. 214.
10. ibid.
11. See Price op. cit., pp. 10–11.
12. Wittgenstein (1963), §66.
13. ibid., §153.
14. Wittgenstein (1969a), p. 17.
15. Wittgenstein (1963), §69.
16. ibid., §70.
17. See Wittgenstein (1967), §297.
18. See Wittgenstein (1963), §81.
19. Plato (1957), pp. 23–4 (148).
20. Wittgenstein (1963), §70.
21. See ibid., §71.
22. ibid., §68–9.
23. ibid., §84.
24. ibid., §87.
25. A common source of philosophical scepticism.
26. Wittgenstein (1963), §80.
27. Wittgenstein (1956), Part IV, §2.
28. See Wittgenstein (1963), §85, and Wittgenstein (1969 (b)), §139.
29. See Wittgenstein (1963), §66–7.
30. ibid., §71.
31. See Wittgenstein (1967), §301–2, and Wittgenstein (1969 (b)), §139.
32. See Wittgenstein (1969a), pp. 140–1.
33. Wittgenstein (1967), §372.
34. See Wittgenstein (1969a), p. 135.
35. ibid., pp. 133–4.
36. Wittgenstein (1967), §568.
37. ibid., §331.
38. Wittgenstein (1963), §65–6.
39. Wittgenstein (1969a), p. 134.
40. ibid.

41. See Bambrough (1961), p. 215.
42. Wittgenstein (1974a), p. 321.

CHAPTER 5   ARE THERE LOGICAL TRUTHS?

1. See Waismann (1950–3).
2. See Wittgenstein (1956), Part IV, 2.
3. Rhees (1970), p. 75.
4. See Dilman (1981), 'Meaning and Circumstances'.
5. Strawson and Grice (1956).
6. In a letter to Russell he characterised it as 'the cardinal problem of philosophy'. See Wittgenstein (1974 (b)), p. 71.
7. See Wittgenstein (1961), 4.112.
8. See Wisdom (1953), 'How does anyone ever say to another anything worth hearing when he doesn't know anything the other doesn't know?', p. 248.
9. See Toulmin (1961), pp. 97–101.
10. See Wisdom's treatment of the question 'Can we know what others think and feel?' and the answer that 'We cannot know this' in Wisdom (1952), and in Wisdom (1965), 'A Feature of Wittgenstein's Technique'.
11. Wittgenstein (1956), Part V, §45.
12. Wittgenstein (1967), §358.
13. ibid.
14. See Dilman (1973), p. 163.
15. Wittgenstein (1967), §130.
16. ibid., §320.
17. See Wittgenstein's discussion of the sense in which the steps we take in developing a mathematical series are determined by a formula – Wittgenstein (1963), §189–90, etc.
18. See his criticism of the Formalist view of mathematics in Wittgenstein (1956), Part IV.
19. ibid., Part I, §116.
20. See ibid. Part IV, §2.
21. ibid., Part IV, §41.
22. ibid., Part III, §5.
23. Wittgenstein (1969b), §103.
24. See Wittgenstein (1956), Part I, §116.
25. ibid., Part III, §30.
26. See Dilman (1973), chapter 11, section 3.
27. Wittgenstein (1956), Part II, §31.
28. ibid., Part I, §154.
29. ibid., Part I, §46.
30. See Wittgenstein (1963), §454.
31. Wittgenstein (1969b), §105.
32. ibid., §106, §108.
33. ibid., §108.
34. ibid., §109–10.
35. ibid., §341.

36.   ibid., §342.
37.   ibid., §343.

CHAPTER 6   LANGUAGE AND EXPERIENCE

1.   Quine and Ullian (1970), p. 13.
2.   Quine (1969), p. 79.
3.   ibid.
4.   ibid., p. 89.
5.   Quine and Ullian (1970), p. 15.
6.   ibid., p. 16.
7.   Quine (1975), p. 234.
8.   ibid., p. 2.
9.   This point is well argued by G. A. Paul in 'Is there a Problem about Sense data?'. See Paul (1951).
10.   Quine (1975), pp. 234–5
11.   ibid. It goes without saying that when I look at and see things, there is no irritation or sensation – a point made forcefully by Ryle in *The Concept of Mind*.
12.   Quine (1969), p. 82.
13.   ibid., p. 83.
14.   ibid., pp. 82–3.
15.   ibid., p. 84.
16.   ibid.
17.   ibid., p. 85.
18.   ibid.
19.   ibid., p. 86.
20.   ibid.
21.   ibid., pp. 86–7.
22.   ibid., p. 87.
23.   ibid., p. 88.
24.   ibid., p. 89.
25.   ibid., pp. 89–90.
26.   ibid., p. 53.
27.   ibid., p. 49.
28.   ibid.
29.   ibid., p. 75.
30.   ibid., p. 71.
31.   ibid., p. 87.
32.   ibid., p. 81.
33.   ibid., p. 89.
34.   ibid., p. 84.
35.   ibid., p. 75.
36.   Wittgenstein (1956), Part V, §46.
37.   Wittgenstein (1969b) §94.
38.   Quoted by Bennett (1966), pp. 104–5.
39.   Quine (1969), p. 81.
40.   Perhaps comparable to Skinner's conception of 'the world within one's skin'.

41. Kant (1961), p. 93 – A.51/B.75.
42. Wittgenstein (1967), §332.
43. Wittgenstein discusses this question in the earlier parts of *Philosophical Investigations*.

Bibliography

Bambrough, Renford (1960–61), 'Universals and Family Resemblances', *Arist. Soc. Proc.*.

Bennett, Jonathan (1966), *Kant's Analytic* (Cambridge University Press).

Berkeley, George (1950), *The Principles of Human Knowledge* (Everyman's Library, J.M.Dent and Sons).

Carnap, Rudolf (1967), The Logical Structure of the World trans. by Rolf A. George (Routledge and Kegan Paul).

Dilman, Ilham (1973), *Induction and Deduction, A Study in Wittgenstein* (Blackwell).

—— (1975), *Matter and Mind, Two Essays in Epistemology* (Macmillan).

—— (1974), 'Paradoxes and Discoveries', *Wisdom: Twelve Essays*, ed. by Renford Bambrough (Blackwell).

—— (1978–79), 'Universals: Bambrough on Wittgenstein', *Arist. Soc. Proc.*

—— (1981), *Studies in Language and Reason* (Macmillan).

Hanson, N.R. (1958), *Patterns of Discovery* (Cambridge University Press).

Hume, David (1967), *A Treatise of Human Nature*, ed. by L.A.Selby-Bigge (Oxford).

Kant, Immanuel (1961), *Critique of Pure Reason*, trans. by Norman Kemp Smith (Macmillan).

Locke, John (1959), *An Essay Concerning Human Understanding* (Everyman's Library, J.M.Dent and Sons).

Mackie, J.L. (1976), *Problems from Locke* (Clarendon Press).

Moore, G.E. (1962), *Some Main Problems of Philosophy* (Allen and Unwin).

—— (1963) 'Proof of an External World', *Philosophical Papers* (Allen and Unwin).

Paul, G.A. (1951), 'Is there a Problem about Sense-data?', *Logic and Language*, vol. I, ed. by A.G.N.Flew (Blackwell).

Plato (1957), 'Theaetetus', *Plato's Theory of Knowledge*, trans. by Francis Cornford (The Liberal Arts Press).

—— (1973), 'Phaedo', *The Last Days of Socrates* (Penguin Classics).

Price, H.H. (1953), *Thinking and Experience* (Hutchinson's University Library).

Quine, W.V. (1963), *From a Logical Point of View* (Harper Torchbooks).

—— (1975) *Word and Object* (The M.I.T. Press).

—— (1969), *Ontological Relativity and Other Essays* (Columbia University Press).

Quine, W.V. and Ullian, J.S. (1970), *The Web of Belief* (Random House).

Rhees, Rush (1970), *Discussions of Wittgenstein* (Routledge and Kegan Paul).

Russell, Bertrand (1956), 'The Philosophy of Logical Atomism', *Logic and Knowledge*, ed. by Robert C. Marsh (Allen and Unwin).

—— (1973), *The Problems of Philosophy* (Oxford University Press).

Ryle, Gilbert (1950), Contribution to a Philosophers' Symposium in *The Physical Basis of Mind*, ed. by Peter Laslett (Blackwell).

—— (1966) *The Concept of Mind* (Barnes and Noble).

Strawson, P.F. and Grice, H.P. (1956), 'In Defence of a Dogma', *The Philosophical Review*.

Toulmin, Stephen (1955), *The Philosophy of Science, An Introduction* (Hutchinson).

—— (1961), *Foresight and Understanding: An Inquiry into the Aims of Science* (Hutchinson).

Toulmin, Stephen and Goodfield, June (1962), *The Architecture of Matter* (Hutchinson University Library, part of Hutchinson Publishing Group).

Waismann, Friedrich, 'Analytic-Synthetic', *Analysis* vol.10, 1949–50; vol.11, 1950–51; vol.13, no.1, Oct. 1952; vol.13, no.4, March 1953.

Wisdom, John (1952), *Other Minds* (Blackwell).

—— (1953), *Philosophy and Psycho-Analysis* (Blackwell).

—— (1965), *Paradox and Discovery* (Blackwell).

Wittgenstein, Ludwig (1961), *Tractatus Logico-Philosophicus*, trans. by Pears and McGuinness (Routledge).

—— (1963), *Philosophical Investigations* (Blackwell).

—— (1956), *Remarks on the Foundations of Mathematics* (Blackwell).

—— (1966), 'Lectures on Religious Belief', *Lectures and Conversations*, ed. by Cyril Barrett (Blackwell).

—— (1967), *Zettel* (Blackwell).

—— (1969a), *The Blue and Brown Books* (Blackwell).

—— (1969b), *On Certainty* (Blackwell).

—— (1971), 'Remarks on Frazer's *Golden Bough*', *The Human World* No.3, May.

—— (1974a), *Philosophical Grammar* (Blackwell).

—— (1974b), *Letters to Russell, Keynes and Moore* (Blackwell).

Index

abstract, ix, 2, 3, 8, 21, 42, 43, 52, 54, 71, 81, 124
Achilles and the Tortoise, 94, 101
analogy, 7, 70, 108
analytic, analyticity, viii, 42, 72–84, 95, 101, 106, 111, 125, 126
anti-realism, 47, 54, 67, 124
a posteriori, 10, 74
a priori, 1, 10, 73–5, 81, 83, 107, 118
Aristotle, 48, 49
Aristotelian, 48, 70
assumption, vii, 8, 88, 93, 104, 106
attribute, 7, 16, 21, 42, 44, 46–8, 68–70, 80, 124
Ayer, A. J., 6, 22, 31, 42

Bambrough, Renford, 61, 68
behaviourism, 18, 19, 122
Bentham, Jeremy, 85
Berkeley, George, 6, 7, 21–6, 30, 47, 54, 68
bound variable, 8, 9, 46

Carnap, Rudolf, 21–3, 30, 109
Cartesian, 18, 19
class, 16, 24, 42–4, 52
classify, classification, 24, 43, 44, 48–50, 52–4, 62, 63, 65, 66, 126
colour-incompatibility, 80
compulsion (see also logical compulsion), 2
concept, conceptual, 3, 4, 6, 7, 9–15, 22, 23, 26, 27, 29, 33, 35–9, 42, 44, 45, 58, 59, 63, 68, 70–2, 75, 82, 92, 97, 98, 112–16, 118, 121, 123, 124
concept-formation, 92, 98, 99, 101, 104, 105

confirm, confirmation, 75, 78, 83, 85, 88, 93, 103, 104, 106, 107, 109, 117, 125, 126
contingent, contingency, viii, 3, 10, 50, 73, 74, 79, 82–4, 90, 91, 97, 101, 102, 104–6
convention, conventional, 41, 49, 77
conventionalism, 61, 79, 80, 126
Copernican, 6

deductive, 60, 61, 94–7, 99, 105
definition, definable, 58–60, 62, 74–81, 83–5, 96, 111, 121
de re, 75, 79, 101, 106

Einstein, Albert, 100, 107
Eliot, T. S. , 37
empirical, 2, 10, 15, 80, 81, 90, 93, 104, 107, 108, 110, 112, 118, 119
empiricism, empiricist, viii, 12, 14, 72, 73, 79, 80, 84, 85, 99, 106, 112–17, 119, 121, 122, 125, 126
epistemology, epistemological, 11, 25, 26, 30, 107–10, 112, 115, 121
essence (see also real essence / nominal essence), 48, 50, 52–4, 56, 60, 69, 71, 94, 124
'essential nature', 57
essentialism, 55
Euclidian geometry, 53
existence, existential, 1, 4–9, 14, 15, 19, 21, 23–9, 43, 45, 47, 48, 63, 69–71, 116, 123, 124
experience, viii, 9–11, 14, 26, 32, 35, 45, 72, 74, 75, 79, 84–6, 88–91, 93, 104, 106–10, 112–20, 126, 127

'family resemblances', 61

formal, 77, 80, 82, 84, 96
'formal concept', 119
formalism, 5, 22, 81
formalistic, 12, 125
Frege, Gottlob, 85

general, generality, 1, 2, 21, 24, 44, 45,
47, 48, 53–6, 61, 62, 71, 94, 116
Goodfield, June, 87
grammar, grammatical, 8, 33, 34, 36,
65–7, 94–8, 117
Grice, H. P., 81, 82, 91–3, 104

Hanson, Norwood, 111
Herz, 118
heteronomy, 2, 82
Homer, 30, 115
Hume, David, 7, 19, 75, 85, 101

immaterialist, 18
inductive, 26, 105

James, William, 20

Kant, Immanuel, 9, 10, 74–6, 94, 101,
117, 121

language, viii, ix, 3–14, 16, 17, 22, 23,
27–32, 35–41, 44, 47–9, 57, 59,
61–4, 66, 68, 70, 71, 78, 80–2, 85,
96–8, 100–2, 105, 106, 110–26
'language-game', 40, 41, 62, 65, 81, 94,
95, 101, 117, 119
Lavoisier, 13, 71, 86–8, 124
Leibniz, 75
'limits of empiricism', 119
Locke, John, 6, 7, 21, 25, 49–54, 56, 68,
71, 85, 123, 124, 126
logic, logical, vii, 1, 2, 8, 13, 17, 21, 29,
31, 39, 59, 61, 72–4, 76, 78–85, 87,
89–94, 96–100, 104–6, 108, 109,
117, 125, 126
'logical compulsion', 92, 94, 98, 99, 126
logical concept (*see also* formal
concept), 15, 29, 33, 69
logical constant, 80, 93
logical positivism (*see also* positivism),
viii, 15, 85, 101, 109, 117, 122, 127
logician, viii, ix, 37, 40, 41

McTaggart, Ellis, 19, 21
Mackie, J. L., 49
master-scientist, 20
meaning, 2, 3, 5, 22, 28, 32, 42, 44, 45,
52–4, 56, 57, 71–3, 76, 85, 89, 93–5,
104, 111–13, 115, 118, 121, 124,
126
mechanics, 13
Miller, James Grier, 16
Moore, G. E., 1, 19–21, 28, 45, 67
myth, mythology, 5, 11, 14, 17, 55, 57,
61, 113, 116

name, 2, 5, 8, 45, 48, 49, 51–4, 58, 61,
65–9, 71, 85, 94, 124, 126
necessary, necessity, viii, 3, 10, 55, 56,
61, 62, 73–5, 77–84, 89, 91–102,
105, 106, 125, 126
Neurath, 12, 16, 100
Newton, Isaac, 16
nominalism, 7, 47, 48, 54, 61, 65, 67–9,
71, 94, 100, 122
number, 4–7, 11, 13, 14, 16, 27, 42, 47,
57, 58, 67, 103, 113

observation, 13, 85, 86, 106, 107,
109–12, 117, 118, 121, 126, 127
'observation sentence', 89, 108,
110–12, 115, 121, 126
observation statement, 108, 117
ontic, 2
ontology, ontological, viii, 1–14, 16, 17,
21–3, 25, 26, 29, 32, 42, 46, 47, 54,
67–9, 113, 116, 123, 124
organise, organisation, ix, 10, 13, 32,
113, 116

perception, viii, 10, 74, 119, 121
Phaedo, viii, 49, 56, 70
phenomenalism, phenomenalistic, 6,
10–12, 113, 114, 116, 124
phlogiston, 13, 71, 87, 88, 124
physicalism, physicalistic, 6, 10, 26, 122
Pinter, Harold, 37
platitude, 29, 30, 54, 68–70, 124
Plato, 4, 18, 45, 48, 49, 51, 56, 73, 94,
100, 124
Platonism, Platonic, 2, 3, 7, 48, 69, 70,
100, 101, 105, 124

posit, positing, ix, 11, 14, 108, 109
positivist, positivism (*see also* logical
    positivism), 20, 72, 74, 80, 99, 112
pragmatic, pragmatism, 2, 3, 9, 14, 32,
    39, 41, 74, 75, 79, 80, 89, 102, 110,
    113, 122, 126
Price, H. H., 54, 56
Priestley, 13, 71, 86–8, 124
primary colour, 65, 66
'protocol sentence', 85

quantification, 8, 21, 22, 42
Quine, vii–ix, 1–19, 21–4, 26, 27,
    29–32, 35–9, 41–7, 54, 67–85,
    88–94, 99–102, 104–27

real essence/nominal essence (*see also*
    essence), 50–2, 54, 56
realism, realist, 5, 6, 47–9, 53, 54, 68,
    71, 100, 124
reductionism, 72, 80, 84, 106, 126
relativism, 9, 11, 12, 14, 38, 112–14,
    116, 126
relativity, 8, 109
resemblance (*see also* 'family
    resemblances'), 46, 49, 61, 62, 67,
    124
Rhees, Rush, 80, 100
'rules of syntax', 81
Russell, Bertrand, 1, 4, 5, 8, 9, 16, 17,
    38, 44, 46, 85
Russellian, 3, 9
Ryle, Gilbert, 18, 19, 22, 23, 31, 42

salva veritate, 77
sceptic, sceptical, 25, 101, 105, 125
science, scientific, 2, 5, 6, 7, 10, 12, 13,
    21, 23, 26, 32, 38, 61, 70, 80, 90,
    102, 104, 107–9, 112, 115, 117, 120,
    122, 127
'semantic rule', 75, 78
sensation, 10, 47, 118
sense, sensory, viii, 10, 11, 26, 49, 51,
    72, 106, 107, 110–13, 115, 116, 118,
    120, 121
sense-data, 11, 16, 109, 110, 113

sense-impression, 21, 26
sensible, 21, 26, 54
sentence, viii, 1, 8, 22, 33, 85, 97,
    111–13, 115, 116, 118, 120, 121
Skinner, B. F., ix
Socrates, Socratic, viii, 56, 57, 70
Strawson, P. F., 81, 82, 91–3, 104
substance, 6, 7, 51, 53, 96
substratum, 21, 26, 35, 54, 123, 124
synonymy, synonymous, 2, 75–9, 81,
    82, 93
synthetic, 73, 74, 78, 90, 111, 125
system, systematic, vii, ix, 10, 12, 36,
    62, 65, 81, 85, 88, 90, 100, 105, 107,
    109, 117

tautology, 29, 68, 69, 80
Theaetetus, 57
theory, theoretical, ix, 2–6, 8–10, 13,
    22, 23, 26, 27, 32, 35, 36, 44, 71, 96,
    104, 107–12, 115, 122–4
'theory of forms', 48, 70
Toulmin, Stephen, 6, 87
Tractatus, 13, 17, 28, 44, 75, 78, 80, 81,
    85, 94
transcendental, 10
translation, translatability, viii, 8, 85,
    115, 118

universal, 42–9, 53, 61, 62, 67, 68, 70,
    71, 124, 126
utility, 39

verification, verifiability, 72, 75, 78, 79,
    84, 85, 93, 108, 112, 113, 115, 117,
    122

Waismann, Friedrich, 93
what can be said/what can be shown,
    81
Wisdom, John, 20, 21, 25, 26
Wittgenstein, Ludwig, 13–15, 17, 18,
    28, 29, 33–5, 37–41, 44, 47, 54–67,
    69, 71, 73, 75, 78, 80, 81, 85, 91–6,
    98–105, 116, 117, 119–21, 123, 124,
    126